A Falkland Islands Story

A Doctor on Horseback

Dr Tom (B.E.C.) Hopwood

A Falkland Islands Story
Published through Lulu Press, Inc.

Interior Book Design and Layout by
www.integrativeink.com

ISBN: 978-1-84753-626-6

To my wife, Shirley, who shared the adventures recorded in these pages. They formed the basis of a wonderful marriage. With my love and gratitude.

Contents

CHAPTER 1
FIRST APPOINTMENT

Interviewed at the Colonial Office. Awaiting decision Receive call up papers for the Army. Then appointed to Nigeria. Last minute reprieve offered Falkland Islands. Can we all go?

There must have been at least twelve imposing middle-aged gentlemen sitting round the largest semicircular table I had ever seen. I tried not to feel intimated.

"Why did you choose the Falkland Islands, doctor?"

"Yes, I don't remember having anyone actually volunteer to go to the Falklands before have we?

"Well, sir" I said, "I thought you would send me to West Africa, whatever choice I made, that is if I were to be appointed

"Well, he's right there, isn't he....what? That's exactly what we do do - we have not made any other appointments since the war began, have we?"

"That's all very well, but he hasn't answered the question, have you my boy?" He took a quick glance at my application. "When you wrote your list of preferred Colonies, why did you put the Falkland Islands at the top?"

"I knew it wouldn't make any difference sir, so I stuck a pin in the list and up came the Falkland Islands" A chuckle or two and one guffaw - they were in a good mood - a better lunch than usual perhaps, especially for wartime!

"Testing providence were you? Pretty horrible place The Falklands you know. The Argentinos call them Islas Malvinas - bad winds, that sort of thing, cold too. No worse I suppose in its way than Sierra Leone. You know where they are?"

"Yes Sir, 400 miles east of the Straits of Magellan."

"Something like that I should think, yes. Well, if you are willing to go to a place like that you'd go anywhere what?"

"Yes sir" I said.

The scene was a room in The Colonial Office the year 1943. I had qualified in April and was doing locum house jobs at Whipps Cross Hospital in Leytonstone. I applied to join the Colonial Service in May. The interview took place in late July. In those days one was allowed just six months in a house job in a hospital after qualification before being called up into one of the armed forces. The favourite choice was the Navy - with luck you would sleep between sheets most nights but vacancies by 1943 were few and far between. The RAF was full up so everyone was being drafted into the Army. At that time, almost a year before the second front many of my friends found themselves travelling from one artillery unit to the next enquiring hopefully for casualties or sick cases usually with no result. We were, after all, still learning apprentices.

August went by and then in mid-September, my call-up papers arrived from the Army. I was ordered to report to the RAMC Depot in Cookham in a week's time. I had practically given up expecting a job with The Colonial Office. Still, I had been given, as a contact, the name of one of the Medical Advisors, so I decided to let him know.

"Sir, my name is Hopwood and I was interviewed for a job on 24th July"

"Ah, yes, these things take time you know. It is a matter for the Secretary of State. Confidential, you understand."

"Well, sir, I have been ordered to report to Cookham on Tuesday."

"Oh, I see....well, don't pay any attention to that. You don't want to join the Army do you?"

"Er, no sir, but there is a nasty bit at the end of the letter, implying things like arrest and penalties, and so forth"

"Never mind about all that. I suppose I shouldn't tell you, but we shall be offering you an appointment very son now."

"Oh, good, thank you very much for telling me, sir. Where will I be posted?"

"Now that is confidential - can't tell you that I am afraid, but you will be hearing soon"

"What shall I do about the call-up papers, sir?"

"Er, just ignore them, my dear chap - don't do anything"

"But the penalties, sir?"

"If anyone gets in touch with you, which I doubt, just refer them to me"

"Yes sir" I said.

There was always a lot of 'sirring' in my dialogue with the Colonial Office. Maybe I wasn't dealing with the Mandarins, but I remember thinking that I never seemed to speak to anyone less than 3 times my age. I was 23.

Looking back in October 1943, I was facing a number of crises. Not only the possibility of either a career or the cells, but my wife was about to have our first child. We lived in Leytonstone and the German bombers were active at the time. I was on fulltime duties at the hospital and far too busy to think about the difficulties I was in. We had married, Shirley and I in Februaury and I don't think either of us paused long enough to consider how we were going to manage. We both regarded separation as inevitable as everyone did - there was a war on.

Then suddenly things changed - an official fat looking letter arrived from the Colonial Office. I had been appointed as a Medical Officer to Nigeria. I was to attend a two week course in November and from the date of the commencement of the course I would be placed on half pay. Full pay was £600 per annum. The first tour would be for 3 years and consideration would be given to wives joining their husbands if and when conditions permitted.

So, I had a job - perhaps even a career. Then before we knew where we were, Penelope Ann was born. The day of her arrival was a typical early winter's day - very dark in the morning. We were both rather panicky when the first pains began. It was still pitch dark and a long way to Hammersmith Hospital next door to Wormwood Scrubs. In our haste to be on our way, I left the light on in the bathroom which would not have mattered had I remembered to draw the blackout. As it was, our little flat was broken into at about the same time as Penny's entrance into the world at 8 o'clock that night and I was eventually fined 10 shillings for the offence. Penny was born exactly as the all clear sounded. It singularly failed to impress her mother at the time.

So now, there were 3 of us dependent on Colonial Office pleasure. No, my family could not accompany me to Nigeria and it was not possible to say when conditions would permit this to happen. I could not be told when I would be travelling for security reasons, but as much notice as possible would be given. In the meantime I was directed to attend a fortnight's course in Tropical Medicine at The London School of Hygiene and Tropical Medicine in Keppel Street. I was advised to get kitted out with suitable kitchen and household equipment and tropical clothing. For the purpose, a small kit allowance would be provided.

There must have been about 50 of us on the course. I don't remember learning anything. I do remember that most of the others were wearing uniform. There was a memorable character, Sir Phillip Manson-Bahr - a flamboyant lecturer with plenty of what we now call 'charisma'. I cannot now remember anything he said. I gravitated towards the few people who were also going to West Africa. None of us had any real idea what it would be like. This didn't bother any of us very much. After 4 years of war, we didn't expect things to be comfortable or pleasant. We just hoped we would be able to do the things required of us. It was hard to believe, in the reality of the things we were supposed to be learning. It was like anatomy without dissection or physiology without experiment.

We spent what we supposed would be our last Christmas together until the war should end, with Shirley's parents in Yorkshire. This meant a move from a little cottage in Horsted Keynes in Sussex where we had taken refuge from the bombing after Penny was born. This had not been a success with the only water from a well half a mile away and no indoor sanitation. This was not the place to start coping with a new born baby. As if to prove the point, I caught pneumonia and had to give up the locum I had promised to undertake for a GP in South London much to our mutual discontent.

Before we moved from London, we visited Griffiths and MacAllisters Tropical Outfitters in or near Beak Street, Piccadilly. This was a fascinating place where on two or three rather rickety floors, old world-type salesmen far outshone the high pressure style salesmen of today. Indeed, as we were totally uninitiated and ignorant of the needs of living in the tropics, we were nearly overawed into buying all sorts of things, quite unsuited to our lowly status. However, when they realised we had no more money to spend than our kit allowance their advice became much more practical and down-to-earth. It was only the other day that the cook's friend finally broke and I had my mosquito boots for years without ever wearing them. Nothing was available then in Nigeria so we got mosquito nets, kitchen utensils and tropical suiting.

Christmas and The New Year passed and I asked the Colonial Office for permission to do a surgical house job. I was told I could learn any necessary surgical skills I had not already acquired, once I got to Nigeria. Then at last the letter arrived. I was to travel to Nigeria on 5th March to Lagos and enclosed was all the paraphernalia of tickets, labels and forms. Apart from the name of the shipping line, Elder Dempster, there was no other identification. I was simply told to report to the ship at Pier 67 in Liverpool. This information came fairly early in February so we had a month to contemplate the reality of our pending separation. It was an anxious time - the only one who really thrived was Penny, quite oblivious of the stresses and strains going on around her.

The last weekend came. I was sailing on Monday. So, Saturday afternoon Shirley and I went to Leeds to the theatre and then out to dinner. We came back falsely cheerful - not relishing what lay ahead. When we got home, it was to be met by the news that there had been a phone call from The Colonial Office (on a Saturday!). Some unidentified person had left a message to say that on no account was I to sail on Monday. The message was repeated 2 or 3 times. The caller would ring again next week.

Next week came and went. No further phone call. No letter. Elation gave way to alarm. Perhaps I should have gone. Perhaps it was a hoax. Making trunk phone calls in those days to a faceless Government Department was quite an undertaking and expensive to boot, we were still on half pay. Eventually the call was made. I was put in touch with someone in the recruiting section. My enquiry was received with the utmost caution. Yes...I was not to go to Nigeria. I sighed with relief. However, the man at the other end, in spite of evident embarrassment, couldn't or wouldn't tell me where I was going. The Secretary of State was about to offer me another appointment. The information was confidential. I would have to be patient (6 months after my original appointment!) The days went by. I called and called again

- then the letter from the Secretary of State arrived. Above the time honoured subscription "I have the honour to be, Sir, your most obedient servant".

I was appointed to His Majesty's Colonial Service to serve as Medical Officer in the Falkland Islands for a period of three years from the date of arrival in Port Stanley.

CHAPTER 2
AT SEA

We leave Liverpool zigzagging our way in convoy en route for Montevideo. I become ship's doctor. We survive a few alarms and excursions but arrive safely.

Even though the official appointment had been made, that was not yet the end of the matter. I was required to send formal acceptance of the offer. So, after a family consultation, it was agreed that it could do no harm to make my acceptance conditional on Shirley and Penny being allowed to accompany me. Nowadays, this sort of request would hardly need to be made, but this was an authoritarian time and there was also a war being fought.

I decided this was not a matter to be discussed with some unknown bureaucrat at the end of a telephone. Accordingly, I informed His Majesty's Secretary of State for the Colonies, The Right Honourable Oliver Stanley by letter, in my very best handwriting, that I had the honour to accept the job in the Falkland Islands, but on condition that my wife and daughter could come with me. Such a concession was unheard of and although we hoped we hardly expected a happy outcome what I didn't know was that my predecessor was causing a good deal of anxiety by spending his time walking up and down the jetty at Fox Bay in the West Falklands, gazing out to sea in search of the ship bringing his relief! He still had another 3 months of watching and waiting ahead of him, poor fellow!

I don't suppose for a minute that Oliver Stanley knew of my existence or ever saw the letter I had written. I had already been told that I should be ready to sail in two weeks from the date of the original letter. I had been told that partially furnished accommodation would be provided but since Port Stanley was as far south as London was north, the gear we had so carefully purchased from Griffiths & MacAlisters for Nigeria wasn't going to be a lot of use. Clearly, if we were to go together there would be a great deal to get and pack. No reply came to my letter. So, with one week left, I rang the Colonial Office once more and spoke this time to a very sympathetic sounding man whose name I think was Fairclough. I told him that I should be in a very difficult position unless I could find out whether I would be able to take the family (small as it was) to the Falkland Islands with me at the end of the following week. Mr Fairclough, if indeed that was his name (it's strange that I cannot now be sure, since I became so indebted to him), said he would ring me back straight away. Unfairly, I believed this to be yet another delaying tactic, but he was true to his word and told me to our great delight and relief, that we should go ahead and make preparations to leave together. This was highly confidential information and would I please, on no account, disclose that I had spoken to him. I never heard from him again but I hope that he prospered in the Service.

A letter confirming this arrived in the mail two days before we were due to sail and so our adventure began. The end of March was approaching when we travelled by train to Liverpool. We stayed in a hotel near the station. I well remember searching in thick yellow fog for an all-night chemist for last minute supplies of ephedrine and cough mixture as a safeguard against Shirley's asthma.

We checked our luggage labels and filled out forms. The labels had the name of the ship cut out, leaving inexplicably only the name of the Shipping Company, the Blue Star Line. This name with magic words on the labels like "Not wanted on Voyage" and "Wanted in Cabin" seemed to us very romantic. We began to realise it really was a voyage, 8000 miles to Port Stanley, a distance probably doubled by the route the convoy took.

We all slept remarkably well. Penny snug in her carry-cot, a new fangled invention then which proved invaluable over the next two months. Incidentally, we never put her down to sleep except lying on her back - small babies cannot move much. We had instructions to join the ship at Pier 63 but on no account were we to disclose the name of the shipping company or of our destination to anyone. How we were to keep the name of the Shipping Company secret, it was plastered all over our luggage, was not explained! In spite of the fog which worsened all the time our taxi - ordered the previous night - arrived on time. The taxi-driver was full of information.

"Ah, Pier 63 is it?"

This query before we had had time to say anything other than good morning!

"Yes", I said.

"Nice little boat, the Columbia Star. You'll be going to South America then?"

"We're not supposed to say".

"Don't you bother your head about that, Sir. Everyone in Liverpool knows all about the shipping here, you know. You won't be sailing today though, apart from the fog, she hasn't finished loading yet. Her hold was only half-full of lavatory basins the last time I saw her. Bound for Buenos Aires she is. She was built in Copenhagen, just finished or almost in September '39. Her sister ship's a German raider in the North Sea, or so they say!"

Even in the fog the Columbia Star looked exciting. Although only 9000 tons she looked impressive enough to us. I had only been on a cross-channel steamer before and Shirley's sea experience had been as a small child. We thought our cabin wonderfully well appointed and it proved a comfortable refuge against the perils of the deep and the Germans over the next six weeks. It seems to us that the rose-tinted mirrors were the very height of sophistication.

The taxi-driver was right! There was no question of the ship sailing that day or the day after. The fog was thicker than ever and the crew and officer were taken up with loading, dealing with agents and immigration formalities. There were only fourteen passengers. Therefore, part of the passenger deck was taken up with a spacious saloon with a grand piano on the port side with dining room to starboard. It was all pretty luxurious to us, accustomed to wartime austerity. The food too was an eye-opener, so much of everything, almost a week's ration at one meal, or so it seemed.

We sat at table on either side of the First Officer. He was late that first lunchtime and apologised - saying how occupied they always were just before sailing, since all the agents expected to be entertained in the Captain's cabin.

"I am so glad you are travelling with us, Doctor," he said. "You see, the Company keeps the complement of passengers and crew to 99 because of Board of Trade regulations which require a doctor only above that figure. I have a very troublesome stomach ulcer so you will understand, Doctor, how difficult this is when we are expected to entertain people, when we are leaving port for example. I simply cannot drink anything at all and the Captain cannot understand why his aspidistra keeps wilting. Well, that's where I pour the gin - I can hardly throw it out of the port!"

The First Officer was a very nice man and I duly sympathized with his dilemma. We spent most of that first meal discussing the different treatments he had tried with varying degrees of success. I felt that I had not really been very helpful - there didn't seem to be much point in recommending Sippy's or any other diet when he was so obviously relishing his food!

I'm afraid my feelings of sympathy were somewhat misplaced. That evening, dinner was almost over when the First Officer turned up having succumbed to the obligations of hospitality. He lurched across the Dining Saloon as if the ship was in a high gale - although it was still firmly tied to the quay. He was so drunk he spilt his soup and scattered the rest of his food on the floor, the tablecloth and himself! We heard no more about his ulcer for the rest of the voyage, but he continued to drink far more than was good for him!

Much later, when crossing the Equator, he climbed on the top rail of the open bridge and, as the sun went down, he blew the last post on a bugle. Watching him swaying, with the rising and falling movement of the sea, I felt sure my services as ship's Doctor would be required, if only to sign his death certificate! This man proved to be a real survivor - he had been one of those released from imprisonment in the Altmark, holed up in a Norwegian fjord and had spent years of unrelenting boredom in convoy, crossing and recrossing the Atlantic. He was far from being the only member of the ship's company to drink too much, but for all that, the ship was run with impeccable efficiency.

The next day we crept out into the Mersey, presumably to free the berth since we merely waited at anchor for the fog to clear which took at least another 24 hours. The weather was then pleasantly calm for several days and we were able to get used to the ship, our fellow passengers and many of the crew and officers.

On the first day properly at sea, I had a polite request from the Chief Steward to call on the Captain in his cabin. He was seated in an enormous leather armchair in the middle of his day cabin, which practically spanned the beam of the ship. He waved me to a similar chair and bade me good morning - then he enquired as to whether I preferred whisky or gin - indicating that either bottle was tucked firmly into the back corners of his armchair - gin on the right, or starboard, I suppose, and whisky on the other side. I thought I could refuse, especially as it roughly nine o'clock in the morning, and did so.

"No, thank you". I said.

Then, without further preamble. "Doctor, I am very sorry, I didn't know you were travelling with us. Had I known, I would have offered you a free passage."

I didn't think of it at the time, but he must have known I had a "free" passage anyway. I waited, he continued.

"I would then have asked you to act as the ship's doctor for the voyage. Although the ship's complement is just under 99, the men always prefer to have some medical help about and we are in for a long trip".

On cue, I replied

"I should be very glad to give whatever help I can, what would you expect me to do?"

"Thank you very much, Doctor, the ship's company will be very happy to hear you are to join us. As to duties...really little...just a clinic for the men once a week or as required. It is usual too, for the Doc to join myself, the First Officer, The Chief Engineer and the Chief Steward on a weekly inspection of the entire ship. Each Wednesday morning.....if that would suit you".

"Yes, of course", I said.

"So, let us now seal the arrangement with a drink....what's it to be...Gin or whisky?"

I felt as though under orders!

"Could I have a very little whisky, please" I said.

He poured half a tumbler of Johnny Walker, Black Label, if I remember rightly...and handed it to me with a flourish. I think he was glad to talk - he had been at sea for more than four long years, mostly on the same route. This meant endlessly criss-crossing the Atlantic to avoid the Germans. They had been very lucky in all that time but the boredom was well nigh intolerable. The ship could do a good eighteen knots and here they were, voyage after voyage, pitching and tossing all over the Atlantic in heavy seas at six knots and the only seamanship required was to keep out of the way of ships unable to keep station. Many of the convoys had ships of different nationalities so some skippers found it difficult to understand the Commodore's instructions. The speed of the convoy was determined by the slowest and six knots seemed to be the normal average. The Captain's view was unequivocal: he thought, with his eighteen knots he could out-run a U-boat or most raiders - with no trouble at all, whereas, in convoy, he felt like a sitting duck, especially as his was often the largest ship in the convoy. In his opinion, the biggest risk was being rammed by some idiot who couldn't follow simple instructions or keep his helmsman awake.

After this conversation, I took a lot more interest in the assembly of the convoy and its station keeping.

Ours was a large convoy, with something like 60 ships all told. Some of the escorting vessels were a long way away, but every so often we caught sight of an aircraft carrier whose presence signified our importance. Occasionally, we saw aircraft high above us but whether friend or foe was mere speculation. We had one Oerlikon gun mounted on the after end of the top deck which swung into position on these occasions.

Just before dinner, one evening soon after we sailed, the Chief Steward came and sat next to me in the Saloon when Shirley had gone to the cabin to settle Penny for the night.

"The Captain asked me to present his compliments, Doctor. I understand you have very kindly consented to act as ship's doctor for the voyage".

I nodded, wondering what was coming next, my first patient perhaps.

"Well, Sir, as you know, he would have appointed you officially if he had known you were travelling. He, er, the Captain, has asked me to enquire whether you would be offended if we were to ask you to accept a free wine bill while you are on board?"

At that time, I wasn't accustomed to drink much wine and

didn't quite understand what he meant, but it seemed a very acceptable suggestion nonetheless.

"Please tell Captain Jones (I think his name was Jones) that I accept and very much appreciate the offer and of course, I am not offended".

I found it difficult to believe that the Chief Steward really thought that I would either refuse or be offended. In those days, niceties were always observed and he contrived to look both pleased and relieved!

"Thank you very much, Doctor, the Captain will be delighted".

"Please thank him for me".

"Certainly, I will do that, and Doctor" he said, again looking most embarrassed as he handed me an envelope...."We think you have already spent money at the bar, so please accept this. I hope it will actually cover what you have spent".

I managed a rather taken-aback "thank you" before he left - almost as though he thought I might yet refuse! It was, of course, a bar bill he had been talking about and, since we were broke or at least had very little money, it was exciting suddenly to be handed a considerable advance of our resources. For when I opened the envelope, there was twenty pounds - almost a month's salary on half pay! Had the Chief Steward still been there, I might well have kissed him! As it was, I rushed off to the cabin and kissed my daughter and then my wife and told her what had happened.

For about a week, we travelled North West - the opposite direction to our ultimate destination. Although the sky was grey the weather was otherwise reasonable and the sea considerate. We took great interest in watching the manoeuvres of the growing convoy and trying to spot and count the Corvettes and other naval vessels looking after us. We developed a routine on board, which included a bridge four or two on the go every evening

Then one night, with amazing suddenness the ship began to roll in an alarming manner. We were playing bridge at the time, and the table, four chairs and their occupants shot across the floor (deck) cards flying every which way and crashing into the bookcase smashing its glass door, I was pleased that I emerged unscathed with my glass of whisky un-spilled among broken glass. No one was hurt but it was quite startling.

For the next three weeks or so all the furniture was lashed to the bulkheads and it was difficult to use the decks with any degree of comfort. It was then that I appreciated the captain's irritation at being in convoy. A course had to be steered, which took no account of the sea only the progress of the ships. The pace became even slower, the pitching and tossing very uncomfortable and waves were constantly breaking over the decks. We were comforted by the thought that this was allegedly weather in which U-boats could not operate

Eventually, the convoy turned to the south, the seas moderated considerably. At this point about a month after the beginning of the voyage, the experts said that we had reached the latitude of the Mediterranean. We saw several enemy reconnaissance planes very high in the sky and one or two ships fired fruitlessly at them until they were ordered to stop.

That same night we had gone to our bunks just before midnight. Apart from the first few days we had wedged Penny and her carry-cot firmly in the bath. (Each cabin had its own bathroom) with towels and removed anything likely to slide or fly about in bad weather.

We had just got into bed when there was an incredibly loud explosion. I shot out of bed throwing Shirley her life-jacket as I did so. I grabbed Penny out of the bath and wrapped her in a lifejacket as we had been instructed. Then I suddenly realised that there had been no blast or shock or any movement of the ship at all and why had the alarm bells not sound as they were supposed to do in an emergency? I put my head out of the cabin door there was no one running about. The ship was nicely on an even keel. Somewhat to Shirley's dismay I asked her to wait while I went to investigate. On deck were interesting sights and sounds two Corvettes were approaching the ship at full speed creating enormous bow waves in the process. When they arrived a heated, very heated, discussion took place through a megaphone. I couldn't hear properly what was said only the four letter words came across with clarity. I returned to the cabin mightily relieved I had really thought for a moment or two that the ship had been attacked. I remember thinking what a good job it was the weather was so much warmer and the sea calm I had fully expected to find ourselves in an open boat before long

The next morning we discovered what had happened, the

Fourth Officer had just come on watch he was trying to wake himself up he yawned, stretched and in so doing had leant his elbow against the button which fired a distress rocket which had made the enormous bang and its star message told anyone within sight "We have been torpedoed!" thus the rapid arrival of the Corvettes and the instant exchange of courtesies in mainly four letter words. Up until then the Fourth officer had been a fairly cocky young fellow; he became rather subdued for the rest of the voyage.

Only a few days later we discovered that half the convoy had left us during the night again we caught glimpses of highflying aircraft and we wondered whether they were looking for us. At this time Malta was still besieged and it was popularly supposed on board that the other ships were headed for the Mediterranean to supply the George Cross Island. We heard the distant explosions later that day and the BBC soon after reported an attack on a convoy approaching the Mediterranean which was repulsed nothing was said about casualties we all found these reports unsettling since watching the ships day after day we had somehow achieved an affinity with them. We were certainly at the time somewhere near the Straits of Gibraltar since it was shortly afterwards that we got our only glimpse of land during the whole voyage, We saw the tip of the peaks of the Grand Canaria as we entered the notorious submarine alley the strip of sea between the Canary Islands and Africa so called because so many ships had been sunk there. Then fortunately and to the Captain's great relief we received permission to leave the convoy. We steamed away at great speed and went flat out for two days or so the whole ship vibrating through the water with a great thundering noise. We never did find out whether as popular report would have it we were being pursued by a U-boat or whether it was the captain's natural reaction to getting his ship back

A few days later we ran out of beer so until we settled down to harder and more exotic liquor we became a much less congenial group. We no longer had the diversion of watching the other ships and their antics. We were left to gaze at the sea and speculate on how long it would take to reach Montevideo. At the start of voyage before the saloon became abandoned, because of the weather, a couple going to join the British Council in Buenos Aires insisted on providing cultural entertainment at the piano rendering such popular pieces as "O, for the wings of a Dove" and such like. The husband accompanied his wife on the piano and she gave us the full benefit of her full throated mezzo-soprano just as if we were sitting in the Albert Hall. There was really no refuge from this other than our cabins so most of us sat in stunned silence which I fear was interpreted as appreciation. This performance was repeated on many occasions until the man was overcome by the humidity and heat of the doldrums. We all felt rather sorry for the Argentinians who presumably were to be induced to love Britain by this process. I have viewed the British Council with grave misgivings ever since. I don't suppose that this couple were in any way responsible for events 40 years later when there is no doubt the Argentinos misjudged the British character.

The other passengers included a young girl of eight brought up in Switzerland she drank wine and spoke three or four European languages. There was also a young Chileno who had the misfortune to find a cockroach in his soup and who made an inordinate fuss in consequence. A typical example of the Latin temperament we thought.

There were only two other passengers going to the Falkland Islands both Artificer Petty Officers of the Royal Navy posted to shore jobs in Port Stanley. The younger became a figure of real tragedy. He was a very pleasant young man probably an excellent draftsman. Only a year or two later he became involved in some misappropriation at a supply depot. He was court-martialled and found guilty. His punishment was to be repatriated and then dismissed the service for what was not really a very serious or dreadful offence but to him the punishment was very dreadful and unacceptable. He attempted to commit suicide on three occasions whilst he was still in Stanley. None of these attempts was taken very seriously at the time although at each attempt he must have suffered a great deal. Once he swallowed some corrosive fluid, then razorblades and the third time he slashed his wrists. After each attempt he apologised to me for all the trouble he had caused and promised not to try again. Sadly and with hindsight his real state of mind was tragically misunderstood. He was eventually put under guard and shipped off to Montevideo en route for the United Kingdom this meant that whenever he was above decks he had to be handcuffed to his escort. After three days out, when he was on deck he asked for his handcuffs to be unlocked saying he was quite himself again and it was unpleasant for both himself and his escort to visit the heads like Siamese twins. The escort indeed agreed and thought there was no chance of him doing anything he shouldn't. As soon as he was freed he ran across the deck, jumped overboard and immediately swam away from the ship. Such an action is almost unknown, nearly all those attempting suicide in this way change their minds as soon as they are in the water and turn back towards the ship. The ship stopped and the boats were lowered but in vain he was never seen again. The temperature at the time was close to freezing so his end came swiftly.

The last few days of the voyage passed uneventfully and pleasantly in glorious weather under incredibly blue skies. My duties as ship's doctor had been nominal. I had made the ship's inspection weekly with the senior officers and had really had nothing to do apart from dealing with a few cuts and bruises among the crew and sunburn amongst the passengers. The night before we were due to dock in Montevideo, the Captain explained the procedure for signing the ship's papers. Apparently, as there was a doctor on board who could give the ship's company a clean bill of health this would shorten the formalities very considerably. I realised that at last, I was about to prove my worth and justify my free wine bill because the ship had little to do in Montevideo than land a few passengers since most of the cargo was consigned to Buenos Aires. . Most of us got up while it was still dark to witness a sight that none of us had seen in something like four years a city's lights.

The Pilot, Immigration and Customs officials came on board just after breakfast bringing the Port Doctor with them I performed my allotted tasks signing the papers and chatting to the doctor. The Captain signed the papers with some difficulty being obliged to grasp his right wrist firmly with his left hand in order to control its shaking and even then managing only a spiderlike signature. In the 42 days we had been at sea I came to like and respect the captain very much and admired his skills of leadership and his efficient running of the ship. In spite of all the stresses and strains it was truly a happy ship. None of this was achieved without cost, the Captain's health certainly suffered. I have no idea whether the Colombia Star her Captain and crew survived the war but they all surely deserved to do so and I fervently hope that they did.

Then the great moment came when we stepped ashore on the soil of a country at peace, it seemed like another world. We had travelled many thousands of miles Penny was nearly 7 months old, Shirley and I were tanned and fit. Even then we gave practically no thought to what might lay ahead of us in the Falkland Islands. We were still only managing to live a day at a time so we looked forward to the excitement of exploring our first foreign country outside Europe.

CHAPTER 3
ARRIVAL

We enjoy Montevideo. Our first voyage on the SS Fitzroy. A strange greeting when we first set foot in Port Stanley

In 1944, Montevideo must have been one of the most attractive cities anywhere. In a matter of hours we were introduced to a world of which we had no previous experience whatsoever. We were installed in the Hotel Alhambra overlooking one of the finest plazas in the city. By any standards it was a very good hotel. Soon we had visitors, the shipping agent's staff, who were attentive and hospitable. We were told that the SS Fitzroy had left a few days before for Port Stanley and that she could not return for a week or so and we could expect to be sailing, if all went well, in about 10 days time. In the meantime we should relax and enjoy ourselves. Although it was approaching midwinter it was constantly sunny and warm. ----- So we did just that!

Everywhere we went people were anxious to talk to us, once they knew we had come from England, they wanted to know about the bombing raids and the V2s. They spoke disparagingly about the Germans and with some pride about the Battle of El Rio de la Plata and the risks their own government had run in refusing to allow the German pocket battleship the Admiral Graf Spee to remain in harbour for more than the statutory period allowed by International Law. The Battle of the River Plate had taken place in September 1939 and the action of the Uruguayan government did indeed bear witness to the Uraguayians pro-British feelings.

We were told about these events in some detail. Twenty four hours before the deadline for the Graf Spee to leave port Admiral Lansdorf the ship's commander mustered his crew on deck on at least three occasions apparently pleading with them to go to sea and continue the battle. It had been rumoured that the control tower managing the firing of the guns had been severely damaged and was inoperative. The very young and inexperienced crew had no training in manual firing. With the Ajax, Exeter and Achilles prowling outside the 3 mile limit it was not really surprising that internment seemed a preferable option to further fighting. A lot of this was conjecture since the Graf Spee had been well out from the shore when these events took place. What is certain is that the battleship could have trained its guns on the town and caused immense damage and loss of life. As it happened Lansdorf took his ship just beyond the narrow seaway used by the river ferries and there scuttled the pride of the German Navy allegedly at the express orders of Hitler himself. Although the crew were interned they were eventually transferred to Argentina then more sympathetically disposed towards the Nazis. It was in a Buenos Aires hotel that Lansdorf committed suicide, reportedly wrapping himself in the Imperial German flag. For some years the superstructure of the Graf Spee remained as a memorial of these events, sticking out of the mud.

On our first evening whilst Shirley was putting Penny to bed I was taken to the English club. It was not exclusively English but it was exclusively male! It was not very different to any club of its kind anywhere else. However, for an escapee from four bleak years of war it was a marvellous place with its exotic *fiambres* and fine glassware which enhances drinking no matter what the content. I well remember trying to play billiards, or maybe snooker and finding it virtually impossible. After so many weeks spent gazing at the sea surging along the ship's hull, I had acquired travellers' nystagmus. In this condition the eye is subject to continuous horizontal oscillations or twitches. Any continuous observation constantly moving surfaces can cause it, so there for instance railroad nystagmus is quite common. Later I had much the same condition watching the grass on the ground whilst travelling for hours on horseback. The net result on that occasion was that I could not focus on the ball and this was aggravated by the pitching and the rolling of the billiard table. The club members were very well aware of what was happening, even if I was not and derived a certain amount of amusement at my predicament.

The maids at the hotel were only too happy to babysit, giving Shirley and me ample opportunity to explore Montevideo. We found it very difficult to get used to the abundance, really superabundance, of food after wartime rationing. It was quite overwhelming when ordering a drink to be supplied with the whole bottle and the makings to help ourselves. When having any drink other than beer we were supplied automatically with *fiambres* which included ham and beef and other cold cuts, a bewildering variety of cheeses and smoked fish of several kinds. Although we had got used to being well fed on the Columbia Star we soon found that by ordering a gin and tonic each there was enough food for lunch. The accounting was simple enough you paid for whatever you drank. The waiters had their own methods of assessing how much that should be

Although we did not know it then, we had seen the last of the blackout for ever. We derived endless pleasure from walking the brightly lit streets, not only amazed at the lights but also by the fact that the city came to life very late in the evening. Montevideo certainly took the *siesta* very seriously. It was virtually impossible to do any business between midday and five o'clock in the afternoon. After lunch, the cafes were deserted until late at night. Just when we'd decided everyone had gone to bed, the cafes, bars, billiard halls and skittle alleys came to life and continued until the early hours.

One evening we came across a green grocers shop stacked with fruit we had not seen for years. We were particularly thrilled to see bunch after bunch of beautiful bananas totally unknown to us since the beginning of the war. When the proprietor discovered we had come from England, he refused to accept any payment and we returned to the hotel laden with bags of fruit. We found it difficult to adjust to the lack of threat from air raids or distant gunfire. We ventured to the cinema one evening to see "El Diablo habla No!" spoken in English with Spanish captions. It was often hard to hear the dialogue because the audience often reacted to the subtitles before the actors had finished speaking. Shirley didn't like to be away from the baby at night for so long so when a fire engine went by with siren sounding and bells ringing, that was the end of the film for us. We hurried back to the hotel with Shirley convinced it would be burnt to the ground, and only to find Penny was having a high old time with her babysitter who was rather put out because we had returned so early.

We never tired of Montevideo. There was so much to see and do. Its coastline extended to Atlantida, the hub of the South American Riviera, with its beautiful sandy coves, pines and cedar trees. We met many nice people who entertained us in their homes. Most of them were English but very few had ever been away from Uruguay. We even went to a football match played in an enormous stadium next to one of the principal hospitals. The teams both had English names. I think one was Arsenal, but I can't now remember the other. The hospital, it appeared, had been built from money collected from the national lottery which was held weekly with El Grande once a month, and then there were super prizes for festival times such as Christmas and Mardi Gras. There was a snag which I was to encounter frequently in the future in many different countries. Although the hospital physically had every conceivable facility available at the time on each of its seven floors, there was only enough staff to provide service on one floor. It was a strange sight to see six floors of hospital beds and equipment with laboratories and radiological facilities all under dustsheets.

After we had been enjoying ourselves for little more than a week one of the shipping agents came to tell us the Fitzroy had returned from Stanley and had docked that morning. He took me down to the docks to see the ship, which I felt was my first contact with the Falkland Islands. When we got there I looked in vain around the high walled harbour and could see no sign of the Fitzroy or indeed any other ship for that matter. The agent was vastly amused and pointed down almost immediately below our feet there was a small vessel hardly bigger than a tug. This was the famous or infamous, SS Fitzroy, all 342 tons of her, looking quite lost in the great harbour. The Fitzroy was not a good sea boat. It was popularly supposed that when she was built in Newcastle the original design specifications required 10 more feet than the building dry dock was long. This intelligence passed to the Falkland Islands Company (FIC) directors who solved the problem by reducing the length of the hull by removing the offending footage from its centre and then joining the two ends together again, this story can hardly be true but the Fitzroy behaved as if it were.

Very soon afterwards the time came for us to embark on the final stage of our journey. We arrived on board by descending a large number of steps carefully to the water line and then crossing a couple of planks to set foot on the Fitzroy for the very first time. I remember too, what a glorious day it was. It was giving us a last glimpse of totally clear blue sky we were to see for three years. The sea was millpond calm, beautifully reflecting the harbour wall and several ships now tied up alongside. We were met by the purser with a cordial greeting and simultaneously by the most horrendous sound of someone in the extremes of agony.

"What on earth is that?" I said.

"What," said the Purser

"That terrible noise"

"Oh, that's nothing, Doctor, it's just Mrs Barlass."

"What ever is the matter with her?" I asked

"She is just being seasick!"

I raised my eyebrows and glanced at the calm flat sea

"In this weather?"

My incredulity reflected in my voice

"Sheer anticipation Doctor. A lot of our passengers are like that. I expect you'll understand in a few days".

As a matter of fact, the journey wasn't at all bad, although the sky got progressively greyer and it became a good deal colder. Once the ship got underway, the outside cabins were more or less constantly under water. It was rather unnerving to watch green aerated sea being swept past the port.

The Fitzroy's reputation was well-founded. On a later voyage, Penny, by then 2 1/2 years old, was sea-sick in her sleep. The Parson's wife was the worst affected person we came across. On one occasion, she was staying with us on the West Falklands and started being sea-sick five days before she actually boarded the boat, so the voyage, when it started, was by way of being a relief. She was a highly strung lady! Shirley usually spent most of her time in the cabin and managed, without being sick. Fortunately, I turned out to be a "good sailor" and on the many trips I had on The Fitzroy, seldom felt even queasy, and then only for an hour or so, at the start of a particularly rough passage - after all, we were on the edge of the roaring forties and the deficiencies of the ship's design were always blamed for her performance. In very bad seas, she would rise with a wave; do a lurch at the top and then come crashing down lop-sided onto the next wave. Apparently, this made her hull bend and cause the ship's whistle to blow. A good story and quite funny when it wasn't happening, but terrifying when it was. So, it was up with the wave, a twist at the top, then crash, bang, bleep! Sometimes this would go on for hours on end.

Most Falkland Islanders believed the Purser - who did the ship's catering took unfair advantage of the situation. I suppose about 3/4 of the voyages were pretty rough. On the first day out from Stanley on the 5 day trip to Montevideo, the Purser would serve fried brains for breakfast, claming this to be the farmer's favourite! Well, so it may have been on land, but certainly not at sea!

As the eminent gentleman at my interview had said, the Falkland Islands were referred to by the Argentineans, as Las Islas Malvinas. This title was actually taken over from the French, who had originally christened the island "Les Iles Malouines", because the first sailors came from St Malo, not on account of the bad weather. It was often said that the fortunes of the Falkland Islands' Company were established by the weather, not the sheep! This was because the FIC had always been Lloyd's Agents. Ships dismasted or otherwise damaged in their passage round the Horn in the days of sail, would limp into Port Stanley for repair. The FIC would promptly declare the ship unseaworthy, offer the Captain and crew passages home and buy the cargo at a discount. For years, some of the abandoned ships were used as storage hulks floating in Stanley Harbour. There were several performing this service when we first arrived. The Great Britain was actually used in this way until she began to leak and it was thought she might sink. She was towed to a neighbouring cove and beached only a few miles from Stanley. We had a picnic on her decks on Christmas Day, 1946 and, although she listed a little, her deck timber was sound and at least some of her masts were still erect! What a pity....we all thought that such a fine ship - a monument to the great days of British ship-building, should be cast away in such a fashion. What a splendid enterprise to rescue her and restore her pride in Bristol. We have not yet had the opportunity to visit her, but what a nostalgic occasion it will be when we do!

Meanwhile, The Fitzroy sailed steadily southwards and after 5 days, we caught our first glimpse of the Islands which were to be home for the next 3 years. Our landfall was roundabout McBride Head, then on past Volunteer Point across Berkeley Sound, with its low cliffs on its southern side, looking remarkably like the south coast of England. In May, we were approaching mid-winter, when, strangely, the wind was less inclined to blow. Consequently, we turned into the approaches to the harbour in calm weather, crept through the narrows, a few hundred yards wide, and there, in front of us was the city of Port Stanley, the capital and only town in the Falkland Islands.

As we slowly crossed the harbour Christchurch Cathedral, dominated a higgledy-piggledy collection of houses running parallel to a low ridge above the town. We could just make out the long low buildings of Government House to the west of town and the wireless masts near Sapper Hill beyond. Apart from the Cathedral, which was built of stone, all the other houses were built of wood with iron sheeting protecting them from wind and weather. Nearly all the outside walls were painted buff and the corrugated iron roofs universally red.

Strangely, I cannot now remember whether the old Town Hall was standing at the time of our arrival or not. Either, it had already been burned down or was about to be so. I do remember a bit of doggerel which ended:

The failure to rebuild the Town Hall is deplored.
And the shortage of roads is a crying disgrace.

Whenever it was, it was one of the most spectacular events ever seen in Stanley, and also the cause of a minor scandal, which in turn, delayed the planning of a replacement. Whether the Town Hall was burnt down before our arrival (we were to leave Stanley very soon) or not, it certainly burned down several days after the insurance had expired. This was the responsibility of the Head of PWD, which stood throughout the Colonial Service for Public Works Department. The Head of this department spent a very uncomfortable few weeks before the Insurance Company concerned agreed to ignore the oversight and pay up. Down the centre of the harbour were six or seven fine-looking sailing ships. These were the sailing ships disabled many years earlier, rounding the Horn. Subsequently, they never went to sea again unless to suffer the same fate as The Great Britain which had already, by

May 1944, been towed to what was expected to be her last resting place, beached in a cove near Stanley.

As the Fitzroy tied up alongside, there appeared a bedraggled group of people, officials and others meeting the ship. They looked exactly like any group of British people at any small port in the North of the British Isles and it was quite easy to imagine that we had travelled no further than one of the small Scottish ports, particularly since the sky was grey and it had begun to drizzle with rain. One thing did distinguish the place - there seemed to be a large number of "husky" looking dogs wandering around the docks. They conjured up memories of Scott's and Shackleton's Antarctic expeditions. Yet, later, when we came to live in Stanley, we never noticed the dogs again.

Amongst the waiting group was a tall, broad-shouldered, dour-looking man who turned out to be the Senior Medical Officer! He looked me up and down - was clearly disappointed in what he saw - and spoke the first words addressed to me in our new country.

"Can you perform a post-mortem?"

CHAPTER 4
THE POST MORTEM

We stay at Government House as guests of Sir Alan Wolsey Cardinall. I perform the post mortem. Could this be murder? "Quite out of the question!" says the magistrate

A post-mortem. For godness sake!

I was so taken-aback; I had to grope for words to provide an answer. Desperately trying to remember where I had packed the Pathology books....I answered:

"Yes, I think so --- er, Sir".

"Good, good, then I would be obliged if you would report to the hospital tomorrow morning. Shall we say ten o'clock?

Of course, I had no idea where the hospital was, but said "Yes" just the same. Before I had the chance to ask any of the questions which burst into my head he was gone. No greeting for Shirley or for that matter for me either! No enquiry about our journey, our state of health nothing. I was less concerned about the social niceties than whether I could actually manage a Post-mortem! After all, I had done very few and then only with plenty of help!

All this took very little time. Shortly thereafter, we were approached by a man in a chauffeur's uniform who said he was from Government House and asked where he could find our baggage. We thought it very kind that anyone should bother with us. We assumed we would be staying at the Ship Hotel, which we had been told was the only hotel. However, much to our surprise, we found that we were expected at Government House to stay with His Excellency the Governor, Sir Alan Wolsey Cardinall, and that, at 11 o'clock in the morning on 19th May, 1944, was were we went.

Sir Alan was a bachelor, and at the time, he must have been one side or the other of 60. He was unwell, having suffered from Diabetes for several years, which, together, with side effects, mottled his complexion. Penny took one look at him and started yelling her head off! So, our formal introduction to the Governor took place.

"That baby doesn't like me"!

"I'm afraid she's reacting to all the upheaval of our arrival and so on, Sir."...I said

Apart from this uncertain start, we got on very well with Sir Alan. However, he remained convinced that Penny did not like him! It was true that she started bawling whenever she saw him, so we did our best to keep these occasions to a minimum. Penny was usually most amenable and so, once her appetite was appeased, we could espect her to lie quietly in her carrycot in which she continued to sleep. Consequently, we were able to turn up punctually to lunch on that first day. There were just ourselves and the Governor, who made a real effort to put us at our ease and was a very considerate host. It cannot be very often that it falls to one who nowadays would pass as a Head of State to entertain the most junior recruit. On that first day, I vividly recall viewing, with some dismay, a jug on the table filled with what looked like malt whisky. I remember thinking it was true after all; colonials did develop peculiar drinking habits. I thought how odd it was to put whisky in a jug and not a decanter. When Sir Alan offereed to pour me a glass, I nonchalantly refused, hoping no fleeting expression of disapproval appeared on my face. However, clarification surfaced that evening when we bathed Penny, her bottom half disappeared from sight under dark brown water!

Peat was the answer! What we had been offered at lunchtime, was merely water. Since the water system relied on surface water and the Islands were covered in peat deposits, the discoloration resulted. It was perfectly safe and potable, (as the experts put it) but brown!

Peat provided the major source for heating; paraffin was used in stoves for cooking and in lamps for lighting in the Camp. In most field stations, wind generators were used for limited electiricy for pumping water and charging batteries. I think coal was the source of power for electricity, since one of the store ships in Stanley Harbour was always known as "the coal hulk".

We enjoyed our first days in the Islands. It was nice to be in a home again, even though it was Government House. That evening was pleasantly spent listening to Sir Alan's reminicences. He had had an adventurous life - at one time he had been a “cub” reporter on a Vancouver newspaper. He had rounded Cape Horn in sail and then became a District Officer in the Gold Coast, as it was then. He regaled us with tales of Leopard men and women in West Africa. None of this was as boring as it may sound, especially to a young couple with four years of war behind them who had grown up in England! Sir Alan enjoyed an audience and he must have been lonely in his rambing official residence, with only an odd official to see during the day and the very occasional visitor. Not all of this took place on our first evening but enough to make me forget about the problem I might have to solve the following day. Our baggage had not turned up, so I resigned myself to making do without the Pathology books!

The next morning, following directions, I set out to walk to the hospital. At that time, there were only two civilian cars on the Islands, one naturally, belonged to the Governor and the other to the Medical Officer which was eventually allocated to me. The reason was simply that the doctor had to be given motor transport to visit the sick on a regular basis and in emergencies. The only other assisted way of getting anywhere, as I was to find out to my dismay, was on horseback! In Port Stanley, most people walked, as indeed virtually everybody had done in wartime England, so to walk several miles or so to work was an accepted feature of everyday life. Therefore, the half mile or so to walk for my first visit to the hospital was neither here nor there. It was a fine, clear day with very little wind; I remember this simply because days without wind were few and far between.

The hospital was a single storied building, with rooms arranged on either side of a single corridor and probably had no more than 20 beds. The theatre was reasonably well equipped and had good natural lighting, although it faced north. The Labour room was next door to the Matron’s bedroom!

I walked through the main entrance to the hospital and met, not the Senior Medical Officer, whom I don’t remember seeing all day, but the Hospital Secretary. Mr Rutter who was then and always remained charming and helpful.

"Good morning, Doctor". I expect you've come to do the Post-mortem?"

After introducing one another - shaking hands and so on, I asked whether there were any case notes or similar information.

"Not that I know of, Doctor. I will ask one of the nurses to take you over to the mortuary".

He implied that everything would be there. The nurse turned out to be a probationer (I suppose now called a student or trainee nurse). She was very young and far less eperienced than even I was.

"Are you going to help me today, Nurse?" I asked.

"Yes" she answered, rather breathlessly.

"Have you done this sort of thing before?"

"No, never, Doctor".

For some reason, this greatly improved my self-confidence. At least, there would be nobody there to criticise or say afterwards that I didn't know what I was doing. We went behind the hospital to a little rectangular building rather like a watchman's hut. This proved to be the morgue! The nurse opened the door and stood back for me to enter.

I found myself in a tiny room, which had only a concrete slab in the middle. No tap or any water supply and one small shuttered window. All I could see in the dim light appeared to be a heap of dirty clothing. I was somewhat taken aback.

"Good God, whatever is that?"

"That's Mrs Brown" (Jones or Robinson....I can not be certain of the name) said the pretty little blonde nurse.

I opened the window to take a closer look. It was not the sort of sight one would expect if dealing simply with death from a natural cause.

"Who on earth put her in here like this?"

"The police, Doctor"!

Oh dear, I thought, so this isn't natural causes. I wasn't surprised after seeing the body, but slightly surprised that nobody had commented.

"Is there a police report?"

Needless to say, there was no report of any kind.

Oh well... I thought...better get on with the job!

"Nurse, could you bring the Post-mortem instruments please?"

"I don't think we have any, Doctor."

I was sure she must be mistaken, but no one in the hospital (there were very few staff that morning!) had ever heard of any. No Post-mortem examinations had been performed for years! I spent some time mobilising some instruments of possible use. We ended up with a few scalpels from the theatre, a butcher's saw from the meat-house, a baling needle for sewing bales of wool, a ball of twine and a bucket of water!

Although it took a long time, somewhat to my own surprise, I successfully completed the examnation. I had been told to report to the magistrate, Mr Cathay, when I had finished. By this time, six o'clock or so, it was already dark. I was told that I would probably find him at the Colony Club. This turned out to be a small house with a bar downstairs and a billiard room upstairs - exclusively male! Mr Cathay wasn't there, but there was a telephone.

"Mr Cathay, my name is Hopwood - I am the new Medical Officer and I have just completed the Post-mortem you requested".

"My dear fellow, how very kind of you to ring at this time of night. Have you been able to establish the cause of death?"

"I think I have, yes, Sir" I replied.

"Splendid, and what did she die of?"

"Well, Sir," I began, speaking slowly to marshal my explanation and supporting evidence.

"She died of Asphyxia", I continued cautiously.

"Ah, good, well done, very clever of you to have reached an unequivocal diagnosis. Asphyxia....splendid...it won't be necessary for me to call a jury. I really am most obliged to you, unpleasant things, these examinations, but we have to have them you know. Just....if you will be so kind, send me the report - no hurry of course. Good night and thank you".

This speech had been delivered at some pace and just as I was about to protest he rang off. I wondered whether I should ring again, but decided in favour of buying a drink to fortify myself. I spent several minutes savouring the welcome whisky and tried to sort out my thoughts. I decided I could not let the matter rest and it was best to strike while everything was fresh in my memory. I asked for directions to Mr Cathay's house, which I am sure must have raised a few eyebrows in the Club, but I was too absorbed in my thoughts to notice. Fortunately, the house was on my way back to Government House. The walk was short and, by the time I reached the house, I had not figured out what I was going to say. I knocked on the door, which was opened by Mr Cathay himself. He was a tall man and, because I remained at the foot of the few steps leading to the front door, to me he seemed very tall indeed! Otherwise, he was not in the least formidable - to look at.that is! He was dressed in a plaid woollen dressing gown and carpet slippers and was smoking a briar pipe - he wore spectacles which immediately reminded me of Mr. Badger of "The Wind in the WIllows". Later, I discovered him to be similarly authoritative.

"Mr Cathay"? I enquired - knowing full well there could be no mistake!

"We spoke just now...on the telephone.....I'm Hopwood, the new Doctor".

"My dear chap, I'm delighted to see you - how very kind of you to call. Just arrived haven't you, can I offer you a drink?"

"Mr Cathay, this isn't really a social call", I began slowly......

"Really, never mind, you must have a drink".

Before I knew where I was, I had a drink in my hand. Now, I cannot remember what it was or whether I actually drank it. After all, I had never dealt with a magistrate before and here was a man of experience and years, probably around sixty years of age, and even though he did look like Mr Badger, he was unlikely to take kindly to anyone challenging his decisions, especially by a very young MO who had just performed his very first PM unaided! I summoned my courage.

"It's about the Post-mortem, Sir".

"Ah, yes. So good of you to undertake that unpleasant task. I am so glad you were able to reach a conclusion. Saves so much trouble, you know".

"Well, that's just it, Sir, I'm afraid it doesn't.....I have no information, but she certainly didn't die in bed and frankly, I cannot see how she could have died from natural causes".

Mr Cathay scarcely reacted to my statement and so, I decided to try harder!

"You see...she could have been murdered"

That did it!

"No, no, my dear chap, impossible...out of the question. You don't understand...we simply cannot have a murder here." His words were delivered with great agitation.

"Well, I am very much afraid you may well have one on your hands now," I said, somewhat riled and nonplussed by his lack of questions, almost as though he knew the answers already.

He then asked......"Whatever makes you think she could possibly have been murdered?"

I then told him of the details I had found and that it seemed highly likely that the asphyxia had been caused by her face being smothered in mud somewhere. I also informed him that various scratches - especially on her legs....required an explanation.

"Well, of course, you are new to colonial life and must find it difficult to understand. However, it is absolutely out of the question for us to have a murder here. Apart from the general upset it would cause, we have only one policeman, O'Sullivan, and he has neither the experience nor the training for that type of investigation. No, no, the whole thing is absolutely unthinkable."

"There must be some explanation", I said. "Where was she found?"

"On the common, above the town. I expect she had been drinking" he said.

I told him that indeed, this could be a theoretical explanation, but that upon examination, I had found no evidence to suggest she was so drunk as to fall insensible into the mud!

By this time, I had lost all my original popularity with the magistrate. He stuck to his opinion that I was quite mistaken. He never actually challenged my findings, or even, which he might well have done, told me that interpretation was none of my business.

Eventually....he said:

"You really have made things very difficult by your attitude. You leave me no alternative but to summon a jury....something...I must tell you...I am most reluctant to do".

He need not have told me that! However, I had achieved what I had set out to do and what I believed, no doubt, self-righteously, to be right. We parted much less cordially than we had met and he reminded me to submit my report, first thing in the morning. Fewer than 48 hours in the Colony and I had already caused trouble

I was somewhat downcast by this turn of events which I found difficult to understand. Neither then nor later did I have the chance to talk to my Senior Medical Officer and, indeed, even though we were the only two doctors in Stanley, he studiously avoided any discussion of the matter whatsoever. The day, which was after all my first full day in the Falkland Islands and also my first working day as a Medical Officer had certainly been full of incident. I was rather pensive at dinner that evening. Looking back, I am fairly certain that Sir Alan had been apprised of my doings long before I reached his dinner table. He did not refer at all to my activities that day, but after dinner, he launched into a tale which I suspect now was something of a parable.

This tale was about an experience of one of his predecessors as Governor. A passing ship had offloaded a sailor, a black man as it happened, who had been found guilty of murder, presumably by some shipboard tribunal and sentenced to death. The offender was placed in the cells (I think there were two) at the police station in Stanley. Sir Alan did not explain how the authorities at the time had come to agree to this procedure. Perhaps, some statute or other was invoked; be that as it may it turned out to the amusement of some and consternation of the Colonial Secretary, that he was the official hangman or public executioner. This august official, who was the Governor's deputy, refused point blank, to undertake this office, and who could blame him?

At the same time, there was an habitual offender in the other cell at the police station. This man's habit of persistent drunken behaviour had resulted in a six months' sentence. Since he was quite a good gardener, during the day he was assigned for work in the Government House garden. It was the Governor's habit to take several turns around the garden each morning (weather permitting) by way of a constitutional. The paroled offender would usually content himself with an obsequious "Good morning, Your Excellency". The day after the arrival of the candidate for the hangman's rope the gardening "criminal" tried to engage the Governor in conversation. Each time the latter passed the gardener said:

"I know what you are worrying about, Your Excellency".

For several circuits the Governor ignored these remarks, eventually he gave way.

"Very well, my man, what am I worryhing about?"

"Your're trying to figure out how to get that dark fellow hanged, ain't yer?"

"That's none of your business".

The Governor continued his walk, the next time round.

"You remit my sentence and I'll do it for yer!"

"Certainly not, quite out of the question".

The next time round.

"Go on Guv'nor; give us three month orf then!"

"Impossible".

The gardening offender must have seen some softening of His Excellency's manner. He got carried away.

"Dang it Guv'nor, blest if I won't do it for nothing!"

The end of the tale was, I suppose, a bit of an anti-climax, although it may have contained a coded message. The poor unfortunate man, by direction of the Colonial Office was shipped home to the UK to be dealt with. When he arrived there, I expect there was very little information available abuts his offence or how he had been tried. Anyway, the affair had a happy ending at least for him, since he was given a free pardon.

HE, an abbreviated reference to His Excellency the Governor used by the initiated pronounced H -- E not he, made no reference to the pending inquest, nor did he enquire how I was getting on at the hospital. In any case, we moved to the "Doctor's house" a few days later.

The inquest took place about a week later, in the Courthouse, which turned out to be a converted sitting room of an ordinary house which might well have been used for its original purpose at other times. The Magistrate seldom had occasion to use the court and no one could remember a previous inquest and certainly not one with a jury.

The proceedings were painstakingly recorded in long hand by the Magistrate himself. This slowed things down considerably. Then the time came for me to give my evidence in the usual technical terms. There were no lawyers or advocates present and I don't believe there were any in Stanley at that time. In consequence most of the questions were put by Mr Cathay, the magistrate himself when I'd finished Mr Cathay asked the foreman of the jury whether he had any questions to ask."

"Yes. Sir, I do." Came the answer forthrightly spoken.

The magistrate nodded his agreement and the foreman turned to me and asked-

"Under what circumstances could death from asphyxia which

I think is the same as smothering have been caused?"

"Smothering can be a cause of asphyxia but it is not really synonymous, a better alternative would be suffocation."

Dodging the issue, not answering the question and a bit over pompous I thought to myself. The foreman thought so too.

"Yes, Doctor, so how could she have been suffocated?"

I glanced a little apprehensively at Mr Cathay - he kept his head down, so on I went.

"Suffocation takes place when there is any obstruction to the respiratory passages, either mechanical or pathological that is, due to disease".

The Foreman was not satisfied with half answers.

"In your report of your findings, you didn't mention any disease".

"No," I said. "There wasn't any".

Again, I looked at Mr Cathay for instruction, maybe help. None was forthcoming. I had forced him to hold a jury and he was not going to intervene now. I continued.

"Mechanical means would include accidental smothering as when a baby is overlaid by its mother, as sometimes happens, in so-called cot deaths".

The Foreman looked impatient, as well he might.

"Obviously", I went on, "this is not the case here". Brilliant!

"Suffocation has been reported where the deceased has become unconscious from excessive drinking or other cause and falls face forward so that breathing becomes impeded. Otherwise, there would have to be the intervention of an external factor such as collapsing walls or buildings. Finally, I suppose". The Magistrate did not look up. "There could be the intervention of a third party and suffocation could occur in some accidental way or by foul play"

This did cause a stir in the court. Mr Cathay looked up, but not at me. Nobody asked whether there was any evidence of the consumption of alcohol. The Foreman declined the offer to ask any further questions and the Magistrate thanked me, rather effusively, for the evidence I had given and I was allowed to stand down. I remained in court while further evidence was being given. None was particularly significant. It seemed that the dead woman had spent the early evening with friends and was last seen on her way home across the common. No mention was made, as far as I can remember, whether she had been drinking or not and no questions were asked. Then her husband, a man a good deal younger than his wife, entered the witness box and similarly, nothing of any importance seemed to emerge until he was asked by the Magistrate.

"Do you suspect foul play?"

The reply was emphatic.

"Yes, Sir, I do!"

This really did cause a sensation and Mr Cathay clearly was upset.

"In view of the evidence, what possible reason can you have for making such a statement?"

"It's obvious; I've just heard what the Doctor said. Someone done her in, that's what".

The Magistrate glowered at the witness.

"What the Doctor has said has nothing to do with you. Have you any other reason?"

"No, Sir, I haven't".

'Does not suspect foul play' was duly entered upon the record. Proceedings were quickly brought to an end after this and the Magistrate in his summing-up strongly advised the jury to bring in a verdict of accidental death, which they obediently did.

We left Stanley fairly soon after the inquest and I do not recall anyone discussing the case with me. Much later on, after we had come back to Stanley from Fox Bay, when the case was more-or-less forgotten, several people told me that I was asked to do the Post-mortem because I was not expected to come up with an unequivocal cause of death. Also, and perhaps more importantly, I was the only one in Stanley who hadn't heard the rumours about what was supposed to have happened. I thought it wiser not to ask about the rumours.

CHAPTER 5
PORT STANLEY

Waiting for the Fitzroy, we move temporarily into the Doctor's house. A period of inertia. The SMO finds me uncooperative.

Once the excitements of the first few weeks following our arrival were over, we had time to take stock of our surroundings. I knew our stay in Stanley would be short as we were to be posted to Fox Bay East, the Medical Officer's station on the West Falklands.

Since 1982, the British public have been well informed about the Falkland Islands. the Press and particularly television have shown many aspects of the Islands and demonstrated in that year the type of country the Armed Forced were contending with in repelling the Argentine invasion. Back in 1940, the Falklands were virtually unheard of or, at best, forgotten. For the first few months, our own mail was misdirected to a small town of the same name somewhere near Edinburgh. The map we had then of the Islands was a small scale one demarcating the sheep stations in different colours, with the name of the owner boldly superimposed. In 1944, the Falkland Islands Companyh (FIC) owned more than half of the East Falkland, from the range of hills dominated by the Wickham Heights southwards. The same company acquired about half of the West Falklands and in total had about half a million sheep. There was then about 1 sheep to five acres of land. The very low density was due to the very poor quality of the grass, called white grass for obvious reasons. To put this in perspective, good sheep grazing land in Wales was raising 8 sheep to 1 acre. Later on, I found that I might ride all day long without setting eyes on a single sheep. Sheep were bred for wool, not meat. Once the wool yield from each sheep fell substantially, usually after 7 or 8 years, it was slaughtered and thrown on the beach.

There were 16 or so other farms or stations, some of which occupied small islands such as Weddell and Pebble Islands on the West Falklands. The stations varied in sheep carrying capacity from 10,000 to 40,000 sheep. During the war, when the wool price had become fixed, a station with 10,000 sheep would expect to clear £1000 profit when all expenses, including the Manager's salary had been paid. All told, there must have been 700-800,000 sheep in 1944 and thus it was one of the few colonies at that time with a positive balance of payments. The land area was almost exclusively held in private ownership and there were only small areas of Crown Land, Admiralty reserves and sanctuaries for birds and animals (not for sheep).

Many of the owners were absentees who only occasionally visited the Islands. After the war was over, one notable owner was visiting John Cobb, the racing driver, whose family owned a station near San Carlos for many years. Each station had a station manager, who often would be a part-owner or sometimes related to the owners. The admittance of a manager to the select group of "Falkland Islanders" was jealously guarded. One man, who had worked for the FIC for fourteen years and become a senior manager, was, nevertheless, still regarded as a foreigner.

In 1946, the population of the Falkland Islands was 2,319. This did not include any member of the British Armed Forces, which numbered over 2000 men when we arrived in 1944. The local population has gradually declined over the years. It was down to 2171 by 1962 and by 1982 it was reported to be only 1800. This represents a fall of 20%, in spite of the importation of contract labour amounting to 400 or so, including wives and families. According to the definition of a Falkland Islander in our time, this would bring the population down to about 1400. This decline has been due to emigration and certainly not disease, of which there was very little. Life expectancy being similar to that in the UK.

One of the great hopes of many people, especially the young, was to get the opportunity to leave the Islands. This attitude was much stimulated by the introduction of relatively large numbers of young British soldiers. Women, not only the young ones, were particularly anxious to leave, and who could blame them? All they had to look forward to was rearing children in isolated "camp" stations with their next-door neighbour miles away on horseback. The only change they had of visiting the big City, Port Stanley, was when they were delivered of a baby or visited relatives for a short time maybe once in three years. So many of the young women in Stanley formed relationships with soldiers in Stanley and the illegitamacy rate soared. Far too often, the girl was left holding the baby. The RC priest was alleged to have negotiated an arrangement with the Defence Force whereby a paternity package amounting to about £90 as a single payment was introduced in lieu of a paternity order. The latter could seldom be enforced once the putative father had left the Islands.

It was not only the young who were restless. Later on, our housekeeper, a lady in her early sixties, had become friendly with a sergeant in the East Yorkshire regiment who had gone back to Leeds. When he wrote inviting her to join him there, she triumphantly showed us the letter and announced her intention of joining him as soon as she could get the fare together. We warned her against doing any such thing (the sergeant was at least 15 years younger than she was). We said we didn't think she would like England very much. She soon silenced us with the retort that she was not going to England, she was going to Yorkshire and, in any case, she would be able to travel since the sergeant had plenty of money. This last part might have been true but Shirley, who had been brought up in Leeds, noticed that the letter came from an address of an area not noted for its affluence.

The prospects for young men were equally bleak. Virtually the only employment open to them was to work as a shepherd on a camp station. This meant livingt in a "cookhouse", with the other single men, inevitably remote from Stanley. They were automatically cut off from any community activities and particularly from meeting young women they might marry. The jobs were unrewarding in themselves and the pay was low.

We had to wait for the Fitzroy to make a return trip to Montevideo before she could carry us to our new home on the West Falklands. In the meantime, we took up temporary residence in the "Doctor's" house. I was not very busy. Generally, I looked after the out-patients and the SMO cared for the in-patients. We saw next to nothing of each other. I visited a few people in their homes but time was too short for us to get to know more than a very few people.

The house we were billeted in (that's what it felt like) had no blankets and we were lent some from the hospital. In the hospital store thee was a vast amount of bed linen left over from gifts of the British community living in the Argentine and Uruguay at the time of the Battle of the River Plate, when the hospital had been coping with wounded sailors from the battle. When I proposed that we should take the blankets with us to Fox Bay, this created bureaucratic alarm. I was told I should have to obtain official permission from the SMO himself. Thus, I had my first real meeting with my boss, who was also my only medical colleague in Stanley.

The SMO was Canadian, large, over six foot tall and wide with it. His hair was grizzled, he had a greyish look about him and the light had gone out of his eyes. The death of his wife a few years earlier had been a mortal blow and, according to his friends, had changed him immeasurably. I knew nothing of this at the time and he seemed to me unsympathetic in the extreme. Thus the formal approach:-

"I have been told to ask you to confirm that I may continue to borrow the blankets that we have had from the hospital when we move to Fox Bay".

"I shall have no objection but you must put your request in writing. You should, of course, have brought blankets with you" he replied rather frostily.

"Thank you" I said. "But you know I was told by the Colonial Office that the houses would be fully furnished".

"Hard furniture only", was the reply.

"You mean we have to provide curtains and all that sort of thing? I am sorry; I was under the impression that we just had to bring out personal linen, like sheets and towels."

He clearly didn't wish to discuss trivialities.

"Just put your request in writing".

He then told me that he had made arrangements for me to tour the North Camp before being finally posted to Fox Bay. This would entail riding to Teal Inlet and on to Douglas Station, where I would board the Fitzroy, to go to Port Salvador and back to Stanley. This would take about a week and, very shortly after my return, the Fitzroy would be going to the West Falklands and a passage had been booked for our journey to Fox Bay. There was no briefing, medically or otherwise, either about the immediate trip or what I was expected to do in Fox Bay. No mention at all of the poor wretched man waiting forlornly on the jetty for our arrival. As I turned to go:

"There is just one thing before you go". Perhaps, I thought, he is going to tell me what I am supposed to do. He went on.

"Whilst you are here, in the Falkland Islands, I shall expect you to work for my personal advancement".

Very taken aback, I said, "You mean I should work for the benefit of the service?"

"No, my personal advancement, in the service".

"I am sorry, but I don't see how I can possibly do that", I said.

"If you are going to adopt that sort of attitude, I shall have to consider sending you home" he said, not looking at me.

I could hardly believe my ears. I knew, of course, that he could do no such thing and he must have known that I knew this. I began to be glad I would soon be on the West Falklands well out of his way.

"I am sorry to have displeased you," I said. "Would you please put your request in writing with regard to your personal advancement and, as far as going home is concerned, I am quite ready to go back on the next boat. We are not exactly enjoying ourselves here you know".

"I think you had better go", he said. I went!

I don't recall having any further conversation with him after this. Eventually there were further repercussions over the blankets and much correspondence when we had settled in Fox Bay. Once we got to Fox Bay, I never saw him again. About a year later, he was promoted to the top job, or least one which was much coveted in the Colonial Service. He became Director of Medical Services, Fiji, coupled with this appointment he also became Medical Inspector General of the South Sea Islands, or it might have been called British Oceania. I remember thinking how wrong I must have been in my assessment of him and how foolish to cross him if he was held in such esteem. After about three months reports filtered through that he had been invalided out of the service and was back in Canada.

The tour of the North camp would take about a week

depending upon the schedule of the Fitzroy. Shirley and Penny had to remain behind staying in the rather barren quarters we had been allocated. People had been friendly and there would be no lack of callers to see what the new doctor's wife was like. Night-time was the problem. At the best of times Shirley did not relish being alone at night, and here she was in this small unfamiliar town which had unexplained accidental deaths of solitary women. To cap it all, there had also been some kind of burglary apparently including the ransacking of at least one room. It was not until much later that we understood the lack of concern of other householders since this particular episode was a family affair, with one brother getting his own back, perhaps literally, from another brother; it was nothing to do with anyone else.

I had met the policeman already over the inquest. Shirley insisted that I should ring him up and asked for the police patrol to keep an eye on the house while I was away.

"Ah, good morning to you, Doctor. What can I do for you, no more post-mortems I hope?"

"No, Mr O'Sullavan, it's just that I'm due to go to the North camp on Monday, and I should be away for about a week."

"That'll depend on the Fitzroy, you know, when she gets around Salvador there's no telling how long she'll be. Still, you'll be staying with Mr Greenshields, out there at Douglas, so you'll be all right."

I still had not got used to everyone knowing where you were going and what you were going to do long before you did. Perhaps, the policeman's investigative powers were better than the magistrate had led me to believe. I nearly asked him whether he had arrested the burglar yet, but thought better of it.

"Mr O'Sullavan, my wife is nervous about staying on her own when it seems you have housebreaking and things like that going on here."

"That'll be nothing for her to worry about, Doctor, she'll be quite all right."

"Does that mean you've found out who did the burglary? Was it someone local, or perhaps a drunk from the Defence Force?"

"We haven't any information to hand as to that Doctor. It weren't nothing to do with the troops. Very well behaved and disciplined they are. Nobody is going to break into your house, I do assure you."

"Thank you, I'll tell my wife what you say, I'm sure she will be much relieved. Nevertheless, do you think the police patrol could note that my wife will be here alone and just make sure they pass by the house at night from time to time?"

"Well, Doctor, we don't actually patrol, you know, there's only Joe and me. And whoever is here has to stay by the phone in case anything happens like. Neither of us is able to leave the station."

I simply told Shirley that I had spoken to the police and everything would be all right. It had never occurred to the staff at the hospital that we would be concerned about the burglary or the result of the inquest. This was undoubtedly because they knew what had been happening and were not in the least concerned themselves. In fact, over the next three years, nothing like these events were repeated and O'Sullavan was quite right to reassure us. The only other problem we had during our whole stay in the Islands was when someone broke into the surgery at Fox Bay and stole some ether. Since everyone, including ourselves, knew who the culprit was it was only necessary to warn him, in a severe fashion, that if the offence was repeated he would be in serious trouble! I added some fairly horrific details of the evils of ether sniffing.

CHAPTER 6
THE NORTH CAMP

My introduction to "Camp" life. Shooting quail at Teal Inlet. An historical ghost story at Salvador.

My first journey on horseback was at hand.

I had no experience of horse riding, whatsoever. It was true, that when I was 16, my mother thought I should learn to ride. We were living in Hythe in Kent at the time. Although it was a military town, it had very limited railway facilities. Later it was one of the first to go under the Beeching axe. I think there was one train each way a day, but not every day of the week. For my first lesson, I was put on a very large horse which happily seemed docile enough. There must have been ten riders in all most of them very much younger than me and all of them more experienced. We set off walking gently up a steep hill which led out of the town. I was a little ahead of the others seeing no reason, as well as not knowing how, to restrain the horse. I was almost beginning to acquire a little confidence as we passed under a pleasant looking brick built bridge. At that very moment, the daily train, choosing its time with malicious care and with no warning, clattered above us making infernal noises snorting in its efforts to get up steam. Then, unbelievably, the engine driver blew the whistle. I was very startled, but, more to the point, so was the horse who bolted as if pursued by rival stallions. He streaked up the hill with his head out flat, totally out of control. In the first few seconds I had lost not only the reins but both stirrups as well and was clinging for dear life to the front of the saddle, which I could feel slowly, but surely, slipping under the horse's belly. I shudder to think what might have happened had we been going downhill instead of up. As it was the horse exhausted itself and came to a halt, stamping its feet, some 500 yards up the hill and I slithered slowly, but thankfully to the ground. I don't remember completing the ride. I wasn't hurt and I was not really frightened, there had not been time enough, but my pride suffered though I tried to ignore the giggling of my young companions. This then was the sum of my horse riding experience until I set off that day for Teal Inlet at the start of my tour of the North camp.

We were a party of seven or eight people including women and children and at least one babe in arms. For this reason, we adopted practically a walking pace all the way to the settlement. I was given a large grey horse called Marquita to ride, I don't remember how many hands they said she had but she was very broad and really quite comfortable as long as she stayed at a sedentary place, which that day, thankfully, she did. I was ignorant of all things about horses and their gear but fascinated by the Wild West look of it all.

The horses were draped with really good wool multi coloured blanket, then there was a cradle like saddle made of wood with leather trimmings and on top of this came one or sometimes two well fleeced sheepskins. The stirrups were ordinarily ring stirrups, though some riders favoured box ones which prevented you getting more than the front part of your foot into the stirrup. One of the things all riders, good or bad, were chary of was falling off and getting your foot caught. It happened to me once only; it's very frightening to be dragged along within inches of the horse's hooves. Fortunately, for me, the horse stopped within a few yards.

The weather behaved well, as it often did in the winter, for my North camp tour. The journey to Teal Inlet, although it took a long time was totally uneventful. And since we never broke out of a brisk walking pace, I began to think my apprehension groundless and that there was really nothing much to this riding business. The journey we made that day must have followed the same route as British troops making their final assault on Port Stanley in 1982 from their starting point in Port Sam Carlos.

We were met at Teal Inlet by Mr Barton. He was much respected, at least on the East Falklands, being one of two or three members of Legislative Council. Barton, like most of the managers I was to meet was 20 years or more older than I was. Invariably, I was treated with respect due to my profession, not my age. In retrospect, I am sure they must have had serious misgivings since I must have been, far and away, the youngest doctor ever to serve in the Falkland Islands. I was obliged to try and give the impression that I knew a great deal more about medicine than I actually did. Everyone relied heavily on the doctor, particularly in times of emergency or acute illness. I don't suppose my efforts to appear omnipotent fooled anybody, but most people subscribed to the conspiracy. Falkland Islanders, more than most people, needed to have faith in their doctor even if it were unjustified. All this a consequence of isolation the doctor could not consult except by radio telephone and this never happened. In any case, there were only ever two doctors in Stanley, one at Fox Bay on the West Falklands where I was going and one in Darwin in the middle of the East Falklands six or seven hours ride from Stanley. Transferring patients to hospital was a luxury often denied to both patient and doctor. It behoved the latter to do what he thought was right as expeditiously as possible. Pregnant mothers usually went to Stanley two months before the child was due so few births took place in the camp. The movements of patients were dictated by the comings and goings of the Fitzroy, which in our early days was the only ship available apart from a naval vessel of indeterminate character HMS Scoresby. She was not; repeat not, for civilian use. Since the round trip to Montevideo took a minimum of 12 days and sometimes a month or more there were periods when the Fitzroy was no help at all.

I was to learn most of this in the months to follow but Teal Inlet provided my initiation into camp life. As always, the manager's house was a haven of comfort in a world of white grass, wind, long horseback rides and boredom. Teal Inlet must have been one of the best managed stations this was reflected in the large comfortably elegant looking house. All the same there was a double seated deep privy still in active use not as a museum piece. Tea was a serious meal with scones, bread-and-butter, jam, sandwiches, quite possibly cucumber, tarts and cake. Cream there must have been. Mrs Barton was a Felton, one of the premier land owning families of the Falklands and one of the few who lived and worked in the Islands. Many of the owners were absentees living in England and so it was not until after the war that they or their representatives came to visit.

After tea on that first day Barton proposed a walk with a gun to see what might be worth shooting. He said it was even possible that we might come across a few snipe since they had been seen around recently. I had lived in London since before the war and had had no acquaintance with rural life since I was a small boy I knew nothing about sporting guns and had performed very badly on the ranges in my OTC days at school. Nevertheless, this proposal was clearly intended to please and I responded with as much enthusiasm as I could muster. I was given a double barrel shotgun it was loaded for me and I was shown where the safety catch was and then we set off. There must have been half a dozen men, guns; I suppose they should be called. In a matter of minutes we were out of sight of the house, knee deep in white grass with two or three dogs in attendance. I was most concerned to ensure that I shouldn't shoot anybody or one of the dogs. After a few minutes walking Barton called across to say we were in the best place for snipe and advised we should release safety catches not to be caught napping. With some reluctance, I complied with this suggestion but this left me more apprehensive than I already had been. I was devoutly hoping we would see nothing. Suddenly, there was a flurry in the grass; something darted just above the ground about 6 feet in front of me. I was very startled, twitched nervously, the gun went off and something plopped into the grass ahead of me. Within a few seconds, there was a black and white dog standing in front of me wagging its tail and dropping a small bird at my feet. To my embarrassment, everybody behaved as if I had performed some remarkable feat.

"It's not many people who can say they got a snipe with their first shot in the Falklands!"

My host was inclined, I think, to claim part of the credit for himself, perhaps on the grounds that he could spot a good shot when he saw one. However, my unwanted triumph (I had no desire to be thought a competent hand with a gun) was short lived. We saw no more snipe, and I don't recall a gun being fired. Then, when we were getting close to the house, a small flock of geese got up and flew across the group about 30 yards away. My companions politely stood back, to allow the Master Shot first crack at the geese. I put up my gun and discharged both barrels.

The geese flew majestically on quite unruffled. One of the others raised his gun, two geese dropped out of the sky. Nothing was said.

I spent a pleasant evening listening to the recent history of the Falklands, discussion about the wool price, the inadequacy of the Fitzroy and the progress of the war, which seemed a mighty long way away. There was a great speculation about the timing of the second front. No one doubted that there soon would be a landing in France. As I discovered later, this type of relatively sophisticated conversation was pretty rare. Subjects of discussion were usually limited to sheep and horses. At that particular time, the war was good for ten minutes, especially if things were going well. Regrettably, that first evening in the camp was seldom repeated in the years ahead and I often wondered how people on their own or those locked into a miserable marriage, could possibly survive.

All this time, the man I had come to replace was anxiously awaiting my arrival in Fox Bay. First of all, my tour of the North camp had to be completed!

The next morning, I took leave of my host, struggled on to the back of a strange and less comfortable horse than Marquita and set off for Douglas the next station, about two hours away. In summer, a good rider with a good horse would make it in about half the time. No-one ever spoke of distances in the Falklands - only time. It was common to say, for example, that Chartres was four hours' ride from Fox Bay in the summer and 5 hours in the winter. Some areas were more affected by rain in the winter than others. Wet winters would cause passes through peat bogs to become impassable at times. On the other hand, winter was often a good time to travel because of the lack of wind. In June 1944 (midwinter) the weather was kind for the whole of my tour of the North Camp.

Douglas was not a family station but actually Douglas Station Ltd and it was run by a manager. At that time, Robbie Greenshields had managed Douglas for years. He was paid very little; indeed he might not have been paid anything at all, since I believe he was a shareholder. Under the terms of his contract, anything brought on to the station for the manager's use, from a grand piano to a bunch of carrots, was paid for by the company. I don't recall having any patients to see during this tour, but I got to know a little about the people working there and how they lived. The Islanders were remarkably healthy, though naturally those working on the sheep stations were mostly young. There were no flies, few epidemics and only an occasional bout of diarrhoea to disturb the normal tenor of events.

At Douglas, I was able to join the Fitzroy, which was on a wool collecting run in Port Salvador - more-or-less an inland sea - which served all the North Camp. The ship had one more call to make and so I made my only visit to Salvador station. This was an estate owned by the Pitaluga Brothers, one of the few places where we came across a non-English sounding name, though Rita Pitaluga, the only member of the family we ever met, was very English indeed. The manager, too, had a Norwegian sounding name, I think it was Christiansen.

Visitors were often surprised by the preponderance of ordinary English names. In fact, most Islanders were descended from assisted immigrants who left Britain from depressed agricultural areas from 1833 onwards. Most of the people I met later, which must have been 90% of the population, had been born in the Falklands. Indeed, to be a Falkland Islander, you had to have been born, or at least grown up, in the Islands. One farm manager, who had worked for the Falkland Islands' Company for 14 years, was never accepted as a Falkland Islander and the peer group was much affronted when he was appointed Chief Station Manager for the FIC instead of an Island-born person.

In 1944, apart from the farm managers, there were few who would not have left the Islands if any reasonable alternative way of life were to have been offered. Then, there were few opportunities for employment other than as shepherds. Social life was severely restricted, social advancement unlikely; the chance of bringing up children to enjoy a better life than that of their fathers was virtually non-existent. Indeed, many of the younger folk must have left the Islands between 1944 and 1982, since the population figures indicate a fall of almost 20% over that period. Furthermore, 20% of the diminished population were recorded as imported labour, only temporarily resident in the Islands.

Nowadays, with improved communication, schooling, television and better radio, prospects for the future seem brighter. Nevertheless, the disadvantages of isolation, climate, lack of social and employment opportunities, and the 8,000 mile distance from the mother country must still be difficult to tolerate. The presence, too, of a large contingent of British troops living there must have as unsettling influence now as it did when we were there 50 years ago. Most girls had ambitions to marry a soldier, partly because there were few others available to marry and partly as a passport to a wider, more interesting world. I may not have had precisely these thoughts as I steamed across Port Salvador so long ago, but the implications of isolation and the lack of young people opting for work in the camp were always lively subjects for debate. So, too, was the oft-voiced threat by Peron, then President of Argentina, particularly in times of internal political stress. The threats, subdued during the war, were soon resumed thereafter. Nobody seriously thought that the Argentinians really wanted the Islands and any suggestion of an invasion at that time would have been regarded as sheer nonsense. So what has changed?

Returning to the sheep, I spent the night at the farmhouse in Salvador, having gone through my usual routine of visiting everyone on the station. If this sounds demanding, it was not, since there were seldom more than one or two houses on a station, plus the cookhouse, where the single men lived. The cookhouse was usually a double storied, barn-like house with a kitchen and large communal room downstairs with perhaps one or two bedrooms off it. Each man had his own room, usually upstairs, and the housekeeping was done on a communal basis by an older man, who also did the cooking. It was only occasionally that the cookhouses were fully occupied, such as during shearing and lamb marking when it was often necessary to borrow extra men from an adjacent station or take on a few hands from Stanley. During these times, a large station might have as many as 20 men living in the cookhouse. Incidentally, one of the difficulties facing a young man was that he could not get married until he had a house of his own. No married couples were ever housed in the cookhouse. This meant that he usually would have to wait for one of the shepherds housed individually on isolated parts of the station to die or retire. Otherwise, he would have to leave the camp and seek work in Stanley, so he always faced a daunting prospect. This partly explained late marriages, men often remaining unwed until their forties and tending to marry women much younger. It also explained why so many youngsters left the Islands.

After dinner the night of my arrival at Salvador, the manager and I were sitting over the fire sipping a rum. Topics of conversation were somewhat limited. Then an unusual clock on the mantelpiece caught my eye. It was one of those timepieces with its mechanism on display in a glass dome; they are supposed to run for a year or more on one winding. We had one very like it at home when I was a boy and I mentioned this to the manager.

"Ah yes, Doctor, a very remarkable clock that is. Belonged to my father and his father before that."

As if to confirm his remark the clock chimed ten. I looked at my watch.

"It keeps good time."

"Always, always has, dead accurate that clock," he replied

"Mind you," he went on. "In my grandfather's time it never chimed at all. Not once. Now I come to think of it that isn't quite right. It was just a few months before he died it started to chime, like it does now."

"How did you get it to go?" I asked, more to keep the consolation gay than anything else.

"I was just a boy at the time, it got itself to go in a manner of speaking, a very strange business."

"What was strange about it?"

"You don't really want to hear about that I'm sure. It was just one of those very a remarkable coincidences. I shouldn't have mentioned it. If you hadn't drawn attention to the clock."

"Please do tell me." I persisted, my interest now very much aroused.

"All right, though you don't have to believe any of it."

"Please, go on." I said

"It must have been 30 or 40 years ago, I was a bit of a lad just beginning to work alongside the men in the cookhouse especially when I wasn't getting schooling, which was most of the time. One day during the winter. There was not much doing with the sheep but the weather was all right for a change. My dad decided we needed another store, just the other side of the shearing shed. You must have seen it when walking round this afternoon, half a mile from the house here."

"You mean the one with double doors and high Windows?"

"That's the one. Well, as you've seen, it's quite a big building, I helped dad lay out the area for the foundations. It was not long after one of the men who had been doing the digging came up to dad with a few bones. Everyone came to have a look; one of the older men said he was sure they were human bones."

Chistiansen paused at this point and insisted on freshening the rum perhaps in order to strengthen us both for the conclusion of this story.

"Well, it wasn't long before most of the bones of a human skeleton had been uncovered, and we set them out in their proper order on the ground. They were all very white looking for some reason, I suppose to do with the soil they were covered by. I hadn't seen a human skeleton before and I remember feeling decidedly queasy. There was one part missing, there was no head. Search as we would no one could find the skull. So we were left with the macabre headless skeleton laid out on the grass where we had first put it, aside from the foundation trenches. Yes, the crossbones without the skull, you might say."

He sighed and paused, perhaps reliving these events.

"My father ordered the whole area to be dug up, but, no skull. There was one thing, though. In the place where most of the bones were found a handful of brass buttons came to light, with a few remnants which could have been gold lace or braid. Dad gave me the buttons to clean. It felt a bit weird, cleaning a dead man's buttons, especially if he had been dead for a hundred years. You see and the consensus of opinion was that the remains must have been a French naval officer. The French had had a settlement here, way back in the 18th century. This opinion relied on the view that the insignia on the buttons was French. Nobody could think of a reason why the head was missing. It was just supposed for some reasons the skull had disintegrated over the course of time. Anyway I finished cleaning the buttons and put them there on the mantelpiece."

He stopped and pointed to the right of o'clock. He poked the fire added another turf and went on.

"At that time, the chime on the clock never worked. In fact, I don't remember it ever working up until then, though I do remember several people tinkering with it unsuccessfully when I was small. Well, nothing happened after that for some months. I think we'd almost finished the building; some of the men were clearing an area about 200 yards away, when early one morning the skull turned up. It was a human skull; all right anybody could see that. Of course we couldn't be sure but it was natural to suppose that the skull belonged to our body."

He looked across the hearth at me.

"Now, if we had had someone like you around in those days, Doctor, we could have known for sure."

"I don't know about that," I said, thinking of my recent attempts to deal with another forensic problem.

"Why was the head so far away do you think?"

"We all had different views about that. You see all the bones had been scattered about a bit, it wasn't as if they had been in a coffin and decently disposed of by Christian burial. No, we all thought the bones had just been covered up where they lay. We found them just under the surface.

My grandfather used to say that when the French were around a few gauchos from the coast would try and settle and raise a few cattle. Apparently they would bring cattle over by boat and leave them on the small islands for a year to fatten and then they would return and pick them up. I think it was because of this that the popular theory was that some poor unfortunate French naval officer had been set upon by a few gauchos and they had killed him. South American cowboys, it was alleged sometimes used a particularly unpleasant method of putting their enemies to death. They would attach the ropes to various parts of a man's body and then with the ropes attached to the pommel of the saddle jump on their horses and ride in different directions."

Christiansen paused and sipped his drink and so did I. I suppose we were both contemplating how horrible that particular form of death must have been I think I said something to that effect to my host.

"Well of course, there is no way of telling whether anything of that sort ever actually happened. It was the head being so far away that convinced most people, because they thought that the head would come apart first and that the rider would have such a momentum that he would ride on for more than a 100 yards. He might too have been riding in triumph."

The picture that this conjured up was so ghastly that, even then in the middle of Hitler's War, I wondered whether men would really do such things to each other.

"There could have been lots of other less violent or gruesome explanations. I suppose." I said, moving to get up from the chair thinking that the story was over.

"True," Christiansen nodded, "though I think it was the clock that made most people believe that there was something strange about the circumstances of the man's death, perhaps 150 years ago."

"What happened to the clock?" I asked looking at it. By this time, it was nearly eleven.

"Well, you remember I had put the buttons up there next to the clock.

"Yes," I said, wondering what was coming next

"The evening of the day we found the skull and put it with the other bones, thus completing the skeleton, we were all rather later than usual. I'd gone to bed early so I wasn't here when it happened."

"What did happen?"

"My grandfather and my father were sat here after a late evening meal, just as we are now drinking a tot of rum and, yes, just about this time too, when that clock, which had not chimed all its life suddenly struck 11. My father told me that they were both so startled they got to their feet and simply stared at the clock. It was then that they saw there was an empty space on the mantelpiece where the gold buttons had been. They were never seen again."

We both sat silent for a while and then the clock struck eleven!

CHAPTER 7
FOX BAY

In Europe the invasion begins. Local interest in the war revives. We reach Fox Bay East our new home, No electricity, 6 horses and a guide caretaker.

Great events had been taking place in Europe, whilst I was still on my North camp tour. D-day had at last arrived on June 6, 1944, and when I returned to Stanley it was to find all our new found friends, following the course of the war with close attention. The Battle of Normandy had begun, and for the next six weeks towns only vaguely remembered from school lessons of history and geography were in everybody's thoughts Bayeux, Caen, Falaise and Argentan. How could we have known then that the next assault from the sea by British troops would be almost exactly 38 years on, very close to the area I had just been visiting? In 1982 it was Port San Carlos, Goose Green, Darwin and Port Stanley that were talked about at the breakfast tables, and pubs in Britain.

Once we had arrived in the Islands, with the perils of war and our journey behind us we tended to push the conflict to the back of our thoughts until the opening of a long-awaited second front. Apart from the radio, (which we then called the wireless) there was virtually no communication with Britain. We knew for instance that a letter from home would take a minimum of two months to arrive. Nevertheless, when we heard about the buzz bomb's which started about a week after the Normandy landings we did worry about our folk left behind facing this new form of attack. Having already experienced in Montevideo relief from the blackout. the caterwauling sirens day and night, the bombs and the anti-aircraft, to which we had become accustomed in London we were still surprised by the speed with which we had adjusted to the peace of Stanley, and the absolute quiet so very noticeable at night-time. I suppose in the 1990s, we would have been considered fit subjects for psychiatric counselling, and the intentions of social welfare officers, but we managed without. We did, indeed think ourselves lucky that as far as we were concerned the war which had been so much a part of our lives for so long was over. Incidentally, it never entered our heads for a minute, at any time, that there would be any other resolution to the war than victory for the Allies.

Soon after my return from the North camp we left Stanley for the West Falklands. I embarked on the Fitzroy for the fourth time in five weeks, Shirley, who, with Penny had been in Stanley all the time had made quite a few friends. So a small group of people turned up to wave us good bye. They knew what we were in for and indeed by this time I had some idea myself!

The Fitzroy sailed fairly late at night and the next morning found us sailing south into the Falkland Sound between the two main islands, east and west. We passed Port San Carlos later to be the scene of the first landings in 1982. The sea was calm. It was midwinter, and we were yet to catch the Fitzroy in one of her really gut wrenching moods. The cliffs of the West Falklands lined the Sound and they were looking almost like a still photograph. There was no sign of life, neither bird nor man nor beast and the cliffs simply slipped straight into the sea. There was no sign of habitation at all, until we reached Fox Bay, a large inlet more than a mile wide, and surveyed the settlement of Fox Bay East to be home for the next 20 months. There was no jetty or anywhere else that the ship could tie up and passengers were ferried ashore by motorboat. Our arrival became lost in my memory in a blur of unfamiliar but friendly faces. I can hardly remember meeting my predecessor who had been waiting for our arrival so urgently we had certainly no handing over formal or otherwise.

It soon became obvious that the doctor in Fox Bay was very dependent on the hospitality and good nature of the farm manager. At that time Wick Clement, managed Fox Bay East for Packe Brothers, who owned a section of land stretching right across the width of the West Falklands from Fox Bay to

Dunnose Head reaching out into the South Atlantic 40 miles to the west. We spent our first night with the Clements since the Dunlops, whom we were replacing could not board the Fitzroy until the next day. We did snatch a brief glimpse of the house that would be home for the best part of the next two years. It filled Shirley with dismay when which she bravely kept to herself.

The Doctor's house faced north, overlooking a creek running east and west. We had our own small jetty and a fair bit of land with a fenced area for growing vegetables to the west of the house. There was no "garden", as such and no trees. It was the barren isolation which worried Shirley for she coming from the urban area of the West Riding naturally had an affection for the Yorkshire moors above Ilkley, but this on the basis of picnics not to live in. In any case these new surroundings lacked the colour and majesty of the Moors.

The landscape, with low hills covered in white grass sweeping away to the north, was totally empty. The house itself was double storied clad in sheet metal. It was square and sizeable, looking for the entire world like a big tea chest with gables and windows. It actually had a proper bathroom with indoor sanitation. There was an appendage tacked on to the west side which housed the surgery and dispensary in a single storey. For the first time I realised I should have to dispense my own medicines which was something I came to enjoy. There was no pink string but I used to seal the bottle with sealing wax in the time-honoured fashion.

There was no electricity or gas in the house and the heating depended upon a Dover stove in. the kitchen and small fireplaces in the other rooms all fired by peat from the "Doctors" peat bank the other side of the creek. Water was pumped up from a well running into the creek by a windmill which kept the tank filled. This form of power was almost too abundant. It was not wise to leave the windmill going at night, so there was a device which folded it up safely to avoid it being blown down or damaged. The windmill also provided enough electricity to run the batteries which ran the wireless and kept us in touch with the BBC. So the wind did have some advantages. Just behind our house was a wireless station and the wireless operator's house over the brow of a gentle slope The wireless mast, about 150 feet high, towered above, roaring and shrieking at us when the wind was high, which it was more often than not, especially in the summer. Once we got used to its tones and stopped thinking it was an air raid warning, we forgot all about it.

In our compound was a small house for the "Doctor's" caretaker-cum-guide who accompanied me on the first part of all my journeys. I was to travel about 3000 miles on horseback in the West Falklands. The wireless operator and the doctor were the only civil servants on the island, which then had a population of about 400 people. I was gazetted as a Justice of the Peace so that I, together with one or other of the farm managers who were also Justices, could perform various civil duties. I did conduct an inquest once but never a marriage. The other houses on Fox Bay East belonged to the sheep station. The manager's house was an attractive rambling ranch like structure looking west across the bay above the shearing shed and the jetty where wool was loaded. There was a small provision store run by the manager himself, which was opened once a week. Anyone in the station could buy basic provisions from it. We wheeled ours back in a wheelbarrow. There was finally one foreman's house and the cookhouse for single men. The total population of the settlement would usually be about 25 including ourselves living in five houses.

There were 10 other stations of similar size to Fox Bay East and five or six substations on the West Falklands. Then they were the shepherd's houses usually situated on the most distant and solitary parts of each station. No one lived on the West Falklands who was not employed by one or other of the sheep stations that is apart from the Wireless Operator, and his family and ourselves.

The first few days after our arrival was spent unpacking all our belongings, which we had brought from England, and many of which we never seen before, except at the outfitters Griffiths and MacAllister's. The food stores and some household pieces had come from Stanley There we had dealt with the Globe Stores of the Louis Williams Estate, which was run by Mister Rowe and his sisters. This was the rival store to the one run by the Falkland Islands Company. It was much friendlier because of the personal touch, and it was a well-run emporium and small business which acted as banker and undertook all sorts of commissions in the Islands and through their agents in Britain. The Globe was housed in two low slung buildings joined together. Mr Roe would walk round with you, making a note of your needs, which would then be delivered in Stanley or packed and consigned to the Fitzroy.

One small bill, dated October 1944, which I still have was for the sum of 2 pounds 18 shillings and 11p and there were then 12 pence in the shilling and 20 shillings in the pound. It consisted off eleven items including two kilograms of chocolates!

There was a discount on this bill of 5%, which came to two shillings and seven pence. Our first consignment from the Globe store was very much bigger, an enormous forty five pounds no less. So it took some time to get it all unpacked and put away. Cigarettes and hard liquor were cheap. Export Woodbines, always very popular, were one shilling for fifty and we had six bottles of gin delivered for £2/19/6. My starting salary was £600 a year, with £20 annual increments. So we were well off. I remember when I learnt the SMO's salary was no less than £1000 a year and thinking that he had really made it. The cost of living was much improved by having free peat, so free heating and cooking, and free milk. The milk was provided free by the farm. The peat was cut by Mr Short the caretaker, far away the most arduous part of his job. Mutton was eight shillings a sheep and beef, which was occasionally available, was two pence a pound. The first time we were deprived of mutton Mrs Ewing, who had come out with us, from Stanley, as housekeeper took the news very ill.

"There'll be no meat for two months!" She deplored very upset.

"But, I'm sure Mr Clements told me we were going to get some beef this week."

"Oh, you'll get the beef all right, but no meat, no meat at all."

Only mutton was meat and fit to eat and eat it, the Falkland Islanders certainly did. Breakfast was not breakfast without mutton chops. Very often in the season they were embellished with Penguin eggs and sometimes seagull's eggs. Penguin eggs were highly regarded, reportedly on the menu pre-war at half a crown a time at the Savoy in England. Personally, I found them very hard to take, especially fried. The yolk was brick red and the white transparent. Omelettes were more acceptable, but these were bright red too. At the back of our house there was a small corrugated iron structure, about 6' x 8'. This was the meat house. Mister Short would deliver meat, hanging it in the meat house, leaving me to do the butchery. We used to get half a sheep at a time and, during the beef period, never less than a quarter of beef. The sheep I could cope with quite well: I would take off the shoulder, then the leg, the best of the chops, and then the dogs would get the rest. The problem with mutton was simply that's exactly what it was. It had no hope at all of masquerading as lamb. Sheep on the Falklands were reared exclusively for wool. To make matters worse, no sheep got into anyone's larder until it was eight years old and had provided its original owner with a full complement of wool. Thus, we found ourselves living on eight-year-old sheep. The sheep that weren't eaten, by people living on the station, were thrown on the beach for the scavenging birds

Now that we had at last come to rest it was time to consider the situation I had got myself into and my responsibilities. I had not thought deeply of the consequences in career terms of joining the Colonial Service. Indeed, I regarded it as a temporary refuge, whilst the war was on which would offer better learning possibilities than going into the forces. I think this would have been the case if I had gone to Nigeria. But, in Fox Bay, with no contact whatever with technical, nursing or medical colleagues, the immediate future looked bleak. I did arrange a couple of correspondence courses, but it was difficult to take them seriously when there was no way of receiving advice or criticism of one's answers for three or more usually four months. On a day-to-day basis, I did not think I would be faced with too many complicated problems, since everyone on the West Falklands was young and therefore presumably healthy. This turned out to be the case.

The greatest hazard confronting the working group was accident particularly at shearing time or when the Fitzroy was being loaded or unloaded. Injuries were usually minor: cuts, sprains or bruises normally dealt with without calling the doctor. The shepherds leading their solitary lives were at risk every time they set off to tend their flocks since with no recognized tracks all the shepherd could do was to tell his wife or the boss by phone where he intended to go that day and hope that if he had a riding accident then he might be found. Everyone was always very careful not to be thrown, which was the only likely way of falling off! Many of the shepherds regarded their horses as enemies which I found very hard to understand. This was, partly because, whenever anyone did fall off and lost the reins a horse would often bolt for home leaving the rider stranded. If he were to be badly injured especially breaking a leg his chances of survival were not high. Some of the shepherds had various methods of marking the track to reduce this risk. Working horses were "broken to the saddle" when they were three years old an appropriate phrase for the rough-and-tumble affair it usually was. Some of the horses never seemed to recover from the trauma of this process and according to several riders I got to know well they all believed the horse would get the better of them in the end.

Only the shepherds habitually rode alone. Others were always supposed to travel in pairs. This is not really a concern for riders so much as to avoid the disruption of the work of the station having to search for anyone who went missing. There were no tracks of any kind, although, nowadays, some are marked on Ordinance Survey maps. The only map we had was a small-scale one in several colours setting out the station boundaries with the names of the owners superimposed. In any case, journeys between stations were infrequent. The doctor travelled more than anyone. A different route would be followed at different times of the year, or when it was exceptionally wet. The low-lying parts of both the East and West Falklands were mostly peat bogs. It could be very alarming indeed riding along daydreaming, or whatever, to find yourself suddenly, with both feet on the ground and the horse sinking between your knees. It happened to me once or twice before I learned to recognize places to avoid. Peat was very strange stuff and there were places even on a hillside where one travelled in a continuous squelch with the horse struggling in peat up to its knees. The temptation to dismount was great, until I tried it once or twice and found it almost impossible to walk.

George Short was my guide and caretaker when we first arrived, and very necessary, he was too. There were four main routes out of Fox Bay and he had to know them well. About the first hour's riding the same track had to be followed to get round the creek then you had to peel off to Port Howard, Chartres, Spring Point or finally to Fox Bay West, the latter for all points south. In the area around the settlement it was fairly easy to figure out where you were, for instance, it took another hour's ride after you had sighted the station buildings to get home. Further inland, especially where It was flat it was impossible when no tracks at all to figure out the way. You could seldom go straight on a compass bearing, say, because of the peat bogs.

Short also had to round up horses from the home paddock whenever I went on a journey. This was not as easy as it might sound. The home paddock was six miles long and it sometimes took an hour just to find the horses.

These journeys were almost invariably matters of urgency set up at a moment's notice

I had six horses supplied by the farmers and I was supposed to ride them in rotation but some of them were either decrepit or of uncertain temperament. I naturally had my favourites. Whenever one of the farmers heard I was riding his horse more frequently than he liked he used to complain bitterly until I retaliated by inviting him to remove the horse which would relieve me of the obligation of visiting his station. These episodes were quite without malice on either side and neither took them seriously. However, any movement of the Doctor was a burden. Not just on one farm, but often on two or three, so the farmers were most unlikely to ask for unnecessary visits. A visit without a sick patient to attend was unpopular and I took to joining the Fitzroy whenever she was calling at a number of West Falkland ports. In this way, I met most of my potential patients without having to ride long distances or bothering a farmer for horses. Invariably, though I had a long ride home. I enjoyed these visits which gave me an opportunity to see the children, to check on any pregnant mums and to seek out any chronic sick This was also a method of enlivening things for me, but not for Shirley, who only was able to make one or two trips with Penny the whole time we were in Fox Bay. Mister Short, (I never called him George) would guide me as far as the next station's boundary where I would be met by a guide from that station with a change of horses Short then retraced his steps on our horses and I would go on with a new guide and fresh horses. Sometimes I would repeat this process two or three times to complete one journey, changing horses was always an uneventful business in my experience. Sometimes we would run on for a few minutes beyond the appointed place, or conversely we would meet well on our own side of the boundary. To avoid wasting time there was seldom a fixed meeting place. Invariably knowing my tenderfoot status the farmers would send the best horse they had available to ride across their sections and although, to begin with, I used to be a little apprehensive that a new horse would be difficult to manage, I soon lost these fears. I never became more than an adequate horseman but, eventually, I could ride all day without feeling uncomfortable. At first, though, and for about six months every ride I had was an ordeal. I asked now and then, what I should be doing to ride properly, and all the response I ever got was:-

"You're doing fine, Doctor, just fine."

Unfortunately it wasn't true. The trouble was everyone had ridden horses before they could walk so they were quite unable to teach anybody. It was just doing what came naturally and, if it didn't, wait until it did which is what I had to do. In any case posting in the traditional English fashion was quite out of the question since you cannot ride long distances like that. The technique seemed to be to settle down into the sheepskin covered saddle and simply let yourself go with the movement of the horse. This took me a long time to get used to as horses are not all alike by any means and adopt a variety of gates. The most usual pace, on firm ground anyway, was at the trot and the horses were trained to maintain this for hours at a time. It was certainly the safest and most economical pace, but it was also far away the most uncomfortable. Nevertheless you can cover a lot of ground quite quickly this way.

The West had an antiquated but quite efficient telephone system which consisted of telegraph wires connecting most of the stations, the substations and many of the Shepherd's houses. A telephone call was initiated by turning the handle attached to the phone for the requisite number of rings. It was sometimes necessary to relay messages because there might not be a direct connection to Fox Bay. My problem was that the wireless operator's code was six rimgs and the Doctor's was five. There was a trying period in the early evening when people would most often send their cables and speak to the wireless operator. The phone was not often used at night except for this purpose and to call the Doctor. It was hardly ever used for social calling for anyone simply had to live their own phone to listen in. In fact, every time I was called in the evening, I could hear the phones going click, since people were curious to know who was sick. When this happened, I often used to receive unsolicited advice from the eavesdropper. Once when a young man married a week or two before had tried to explain his wife's stomach ache a voice interrupted with.

"She's in labour, Doctor!"

So she was!

We often sat by the fire, in the winter especially, listening anxiously to the telephone ringing and trying to count the rings. There always seemed to be a pause after five rings just to keep us on tenterhooks before it would ring reluctantly for the sixth and let us off the hook!

The telephone lines were maintained by sheep stations and there were no telephone bills

CHAPTER 8
A LONG RIDE

My first and longest ever journey. Travel through snow to Pebble Island. I arrive worse than the patient. Meet the Pole-Evans family in Port Howard.

As it happens, my first call didn't come by telephone but by wireless. After we had been in Fox Bay about a week or 10 days, the wireless operator, early one morning rang to say there was a radio message for me from Charlie Robertson on Pebble Island, about a patient, and would I go up to the wireless station. It turned out that one of the wives on the island was seriously ill with what sounded like pneumonia and what were they to do. I was, of course, unfamiliar with the procedure of making a visit of this kind and I only knew vaguely where Pebble Island was. I thought I simply had to show my patients and potential patients that I really was available so I said I would go at once! I soon discovered it was a good deal easier said than done. The first thing was to arrange Short to collect and saddle the horses. By this time I'd realised that Pebble Island was literally as far away as I could get on the West. It would be necessary to pass through Port Howard, the settlement for the Waldron Estate and I would be away several days.

There really wasn't a problem about what medicines to take since my resources in that respect were very limited. I had no sulphonamides and penicillin was not yet in common use. I packed what I thought I might need into saddlebags, called *maletas*. All horse gear was referred to by its Spanish name since horses and tackle came from Argentina. I left the arrangements for horses and guides to meet me at the boundaries to the wireless operator. After about an hour and a half we were ready to go. This was the second time, I had left Shirley behind and this time she had no one for company except Penny and the housekeeper. There were no neighbours or potential friends, as there had been in Stanley. Everyone In Fox Bay was far too busy for social interchange during the day and to venture out at night was simply not thought of.

It was a: cold raw sort of day with occasional snowflakes in the wind. By now, we were more or less in midwinter. I had dressed up in New Zealand oilskins with a Sou'wester - type hat. By the time I had finished, with extra underclothing and boots I looked twice my normal size and must have been quite a sight to behold. Mounting the horse in this getup was quite a performance. The first horse I rode from Fox Bay was a skinny looking creature which clearly did not appreciate having to carry my weight and the *maletas*. The poor horse didn't have the strength to give a lot of trouble so it settled for a policy of non-cooperation, which was all the more irritating since I was unfamiliar with signals the horse could interpret. At any rate, a somewhat fractious start took my mind off the discomfort of riding for a little while at least. We proceeded slowly, half walk and half trot, with every so often a slithering lurch as we negotiated the peat swamps north of Fox Bay.

We had left at about 9:30 a.m., our progress was slow, and so it was more than three hours before we met the guide from Port Howard who was to take me on to the settlement. It was a marvellous feeling getting off the horse and sitting down or doing anything as a change from the constant jarring and rubbing of the unfamiliar movements of the horse. Meeting the guide was a blessed opportunity to eat the sandwiches I had brought with me, not because I was hungry, but to prolong the rest from riding, if you could call it that.

It was the custom to travel with a bottle of rum, which was shared between me and the guide. At each stop to open a gate. (The stations were all well fenced) Short or whoever was doing the job would drag a bottle of rum out of his pocket take a swig and wiping the bottle top under his arm would lift up the bottle and say.

"Tot, Doctor?"

To begin with, I primly refused these offers, but before very long my puritan instincts faded and I was looking forward to the next gate. The other solace on these journeys was cigarettes. Once I had mastered the art of lighting a cigarette on horseback a packet of 50 lasted no time at all. When the wind was up it would blow the cigarette away as soon as you began to draw on it.

The rendezvous on that first day was somewhere near an almost unidentifiable shack called I think Black Shanty. I was horrified to find that after travelling all morning I was still barely halfway to Port Howard. I remember watching Short's retreating back, as he set off home, fervently wishing I was able to go with him. The next part of the journey was sheer hell, the new horse was no improvement on the previous one, and I recall offering up a prayer every time the horse stopped for it never to start again. . The only way I thought I could cope was by trying to shut everything out and pretend nothing was happening. It didn't work. After another three or four hours, which seemed to last all day, we came in sight of Port Howard under the lee of the Hornby Mountains. I prepared myself to meet the master of Port Howard Mr Pole-Evans he was the champion of the West and the Island's only member of the Legislative Council. I had heard about him when I was staying at government house, his appointment to the council was an attempt to curb his constant criticism of the government's policy. It didn't seem to have that effect. I don't recall his first name. His peers called him Pole, so there might have been no hyphen. He presented an irascible front and to put it mildly he enjoyed an argument. He was Welsh of course and proud of it. At that time, he must have been in the second half of his 50s, a man of middle height with a quiff of hair above a mobile face which could be wonderfully expressive. He welcomed me warmly and offered tea, which was set out in the living room on a low table presided over by Mrs Pole-Evans in front of a roaring fire. It was miraculously relaxing and I almost forgot the purpose of my visit and the discomfort of the journey, after two or three cups of tea. Then Pole-Evans got to his feet,

"I expect, you'll be wanting to get on, Doctor, there's not a lot of daylight left this time of the year, and you have a long ride ahead."

My heart sank, I had not really expected to stop at Port Howard, but the darkening and low clouded sky outside and the warm glowing comfort inside had raised my hopes of a reprieve.

It was not to be and thinking of the patient, and my need to create at least the impression that I would always do what I could for sick people, there was no way I could chicken out. Certainly not in the Pole Evans house. I put as brave a face on it as I could muster and prepared myself for the next leg of the journey.

"You must stay with us for the night, Doctor," said .Pole-Evans. Was there still hope?

"On your way back," he added

"Thank you. I would really like that,"

I replied thinking that if only I could stay right there and then I would like it a whole lot more.

So the worst part of the journey began. It was by now, past five o'clock, getting dark, and a good deal colder, but there still wasn't too much wind. I struggled onto the back of the third horse I had ridden that day and, with a new guide, we turned North leaving Mount D'Arcy to the west. Very soon it was pitch dark. In the Falklands pitch dark was really so since there were no reflections from metropolitan areas to light up the sky so I could see practically nothing. After a while my guide and I got separated, my horse kept moving slowly on. I didn't mind that at all because it meant I didn't have to try and match the guide's pace. I could hear him careering about, quite a long way away, looking for me I supposed. After what seemed to me a long time my horse came to a standstill.

The guide was shouting "Doctor! Doctor!" At the top of his voice and it wasn't until he had nearly found me that I shouted in reply. The blessed rest was over.

"I thought I had lost you, Doctor, but I see you've found your way all right."

Then I realised that the horse had kept diligently to whatever track he knew and we were halted just in front of a gate in the fence. I was so tired and sore all over that the rest of the journey was a nightmarish dream. I was to be picked up on the north side of Port Purvis by the launch from Pebble Island. The last stretch of the journey was along the precipitous slopes of Mount Darcy, crossing stony strips of screes, the remnants of some long gone glacier. The stones slipping across one another, made the traverse rather treacherous for the horse, but it could only be crossed slowly thank goodness. Then, of course, the snow which had threatened to fall all day decided that now was the time to cause maximum inconvenience and came down thickly. At least this made the ground easier to see but also increased my concern, making me more conscious than ever of the horse's scrambling efforts to remain on all fours among the loose stones and rocks. Then all of a sudden, the ordeal came to an end. The horse stopped. I could see the outline of a boat, a converted Admiral's barge, and then the guide's voice.

"We are here, Doctor!"

I was speechless. Apart from a few grunted greetings and thanks. It was in silence that I was gently lifted off the horse and helped into the cabin, where after yet another tot of rum, I lay full length on the bunk, feeling more thankful than I ever remember. It was getting on for 10 o'clock before we got underway. By then I had been travelling more than 12 hours most of the time in abject misery, perched on horses I felt I simply could never get used to riding. The terrible thought came to me that I should have to return the same way. Then perhaps the rum took over and I dozed off, thinking sufficient unto the day, and just enjoyed the sheer luxury of lying down.

It took more than an hour to complete the sea journey to Pebble Island. I shall never forget my reception. Here was a giant of a man looming out of the darkness on the jetty above the boat, waving an oil lamp and in front of his black beetling eyebrows, lugubrious face for all the world like one of the Peggottys from Dickensian Yarmouth. He was wearing oilskins surmounted by a sou'wester, which caused some of the effect, since he never again seemed quite so large. This was Charlie Robertson, who later moved to Port Stephens as far south on the West Falklands as Pebble Island was north. He greeted me with friendliness in his voice,

"Welcome to Pebble Island, Doctor, you will be glad to hear that the patient is much better, and she's gone off to sleep."

So, that was what I had suffered all day for! I felt like saying, well, you can bloody well wake her up again. However, I did say,

"Just the same I think I will make sure she is all right for the night."

And so I did. True enough, she was clearly doing well and I did not wake her. It was after midnight before I got to my room and then I had to endure the painful business of getting undressed. My trousers were stuck to the inside of my thighs, from the blood blisters that had burst. I thought ruefully that actually I was worse off than the patient I had come to see. A bath in lukewarm water was all I could bear, so thus to bed in yet another very comfortable farmhouse. I was a guest of the Robertsons.

The farm managers, invariably, surrounded themselves with considerably domestic comfort, presumably to offset the rigours of their working lives. The Falkland Islands were a man's country and I always felt sorry for the women, my own wife included, for having to put up with the unvarying domesticity of their lives. I don't believe this can have altered all that much. True, wireless reception will be better and television, video and DVDs will have added a further dimension to life, but all the social restrictions we had to put up with probably still remain.

I spent several pleasant days with the Robertsons, who were very good company and, when I could forget that I had to return on a horse, I enjoyed myself. I saw the patient twice a day and visited all the families on the station. The weather changed little and was still cold and west, so as always in winter there was little going on apart from a rather desultory make and mend. We talked a little about the war; but most of the time, we read books in front of peat fires. It's strange, but I do not remember the patient's name, perhaps because she made an uneventful and complete recovery. All I had to do was to make sure she sufficiently recovered for me to leave!

As a matter of fact, no journey was ever quite so long or as painful as that first trip to Pebble Island. My wounds from the outward ride had not quite healed, but I wore my pyjamas under my trousers on the return trip and this helped. I remained uncomfortable on horseback for at least six months but, in spite of my original fears, after that I was able to ride all day without even feeling stiff. I never discovered what it was that I did differently - perhaps I just got used to it - but believe it or not, I came close to prefer faster horses! I was really quite pleased with myself once I arrived back at Port Howard and, since I had started late, I spent the night with the Pole-Evans and met their two sons, Douglas and Tony. Whilst we were having a drink before dinner that night, the old man turned to me and said:

"Well, Doctor, I do believe we'll make a Falkland Islander out of you one day! Do you know you are the first Doctor we have ever had who has ridden from Fox Bay to Pebble in one day?"

"Why didn't you tell me that when I was here before?" His eyes twinkled as he looked at me and laughingly said: "Had I done so, you might not have become the first Doctor to do the journey in one day."

Chapter 9
Whooping Cough And Wild Life

A Whooping cough epidemic. Our movement restricted. We watch penguins, seals and a whale.

After my return from Pebble Island, we settled down to a monotonous regime largely unaffected by world events or, indeed, anything outside Fox Bay. This was the result of poor communications. True, the BBC was a great standby, but there were only two or three hours in the evening when reception was adequate, and we could listen to Radio Newsreel or the Robinson Family at War. Both helped to keep us in touch with the rest of the world and the war however tenuously. The focus of our lives became the movements of the Fitzroy, because it brought mail, news, stores and even sometimes people. We usually knew where the ship was at any one time, but, during the next 18 months, she spent three months having a refit and ran aground at least twice, so there were sometimes very long intervals between deliveries of mail.

As far as my job was concerned, all I had to do was be there. There was no question of holding regular surgeries. Outpatient service would only have been available to the folk in Fox Bay East and everyone knew that they only had to call at the house whenever they needed help. The people living on the other side of the Bay seldom visited. This was only an hour's ride away, and about the same by boat but the risk of a storm blowing up once you crossed to the other side was always in your mind. There was a small jetty at the creek immediately in front of the house, with a fairly large pram dinghy alongside, I used to row across, occasionally, and it was good exercise for an hour or so depending on the wind and tide. To me this was preferable to riding round which took about the same time but of course the horse had to be collected from the paddock which could easily take another hour.

We seldom used the horses for anything other than visits to patients, since this meant getting them and taking up the caretaker's time, which he would, naturally, claim should be devoted to cutting peat! In this, he would be supported by the farmers who took the view that the horses were there for the doctor to ride only when it was needed. They didn't seem to think that the horses needed exercising, and certainly most of them were close to the end of their working lives. Anyhow, I disliked riding and much preferred rowing and I could sometimes take the family as well. Tom Gilruth (who became FIC camp manager) and his wife came to Fox Bay West about the same time that we arrived at Fox Bay East, and we visited them from time to time. Visits to the other side were infrequent made sometimes to see a patient or to find things in their store, which we didn't have in ours.

Everyone suffered the same monotony, especially in the winter when the work load was reduced. The men in the cookhouse countered this by drinking excessively and this sometimes led to trouble. Generally there was quite a high incidence of alcoholism and Delirium Tremens. It was not always possible, even with rationing booze to restrict intake, say to one bottle a weekend, Even in the cookhouse there were teetotallers or others prepared or coerced to hand over their rations.

One Sunday morning, very early, Tom Gilruth from Fox Bay West rang to say that one of the men in the cookhouse was bleeding very badly from a cut on his head. I said I would come at once, collected the things I thought I might need, and rowed to the other side. When I was nearing their jetty, I heard a lot of shouting and then, to my horror, a man on horseback came galloping along the jetty to meet me. I thought he must surely take off and land in the sea. But then within a yard or so of the end of the jetty he put the horse up on its hind legs and swung it right about-turn like a circus performer. To my mounting alarm he did this several times before I got ashore. The man was roaring drunk, cursing and swearing in the most fluent manner quite oblivious to the blood streaming from his left ear, which he had covered in cigarette papers in a vain attempt to stem the flow. It was easier to control the horse than the man but eventually with the assistance of the foreman and a couple of others he was removed from the horse and persuaded to accept treatment. Putting in a few stitches wasn't too difficult but keeping them there and keeping the dressing on was impossible. Short of rendering the man unconscious, and I had not brought the wherewithal for that there was nothing to be done but let him go as he was. He leapt back onto his horse and after a few flourishes he careered off saying he would ride to Spring Point four hours ride away. I consoled myself with the thought that the bleeding would stop eventually; there was nothing else I could do. He came to no harm.

In this particular instance, the man had acquired treble his ration of rum and had been drinking all night with undiminished enthusiasm. As the night wore on, the noise he made and the general disturbance became less and less acceptable. Eventually one of the other men decided, enough was enough, simply picked up a bottle and bashed him over the head with it. There was enough force to split the ear, but not the scalp, so the blow merely served to aggravate the situation. It never occurred to anyone at the time to do anything about this sort of thing. I was probably more disturbed by this incident than anybody else, I had not appreciated that alcoholism was common. Drunkenness actually was not as common as it was in Stanley, since the remedy in the stations was just to cut off supplies of liquor, to everybody if necessary.

I hadn't thought about Fox Bay for years yet while writing this as so often happens, I read a piece about it in the Times. This was an article entitled "Falklanders begin life without the Company." In 1944 the Falkland Island Company (FIC) had recently acquired Fox Bay West and sometime later they took over Port Stephens, so the company owned the southern half of the West Falklands to match its holding on the East Falklands. The FIC provided the ship to pick up the wool clip and were the chief importers of farm supplies. They also ran a ship chandlers business, provided insurance and similar services. The Company was an integral part of the everyday life of the Islands and although the shareholders were in England, the local general manager had lived in Stanley for years. It was true that the Board of Directors was established in London, as was the Managing Director but a better example of absentee landlords was provided by some of the other stations, whose owners lived in the UK and never visited at all and thus were totally remote from running the day-to-day farm business.

In those days there was no thought that the land would ever be divided since, with a sheep carrying capacity of 1 sheep to 5 acres the optimal size was considered to be 40,000 sheep. It is interesting that the Falkland Islands Development Corporation, under whose auspices apparently the land has been subdivided is reported to recommend that a unit of 5-6000 sheep is the optimum. According to this article such a unit would cost £110,000. In 1944 it was generally supposed that for each 10,000 sheep an owner would clear £1000 per annum. (Remember that that was what the senior medical officer was paid) having paid outgoings including wages and the manager's salary. The net return of the Waldron Estate would have been about £4000 a year, which was very good indeed for those days, this was only reached when the price of wool was high. During the war wool was held at a fixed price, but when it was over man-made fibres started coming in and the price dropped. In 1987, the date of the article, the smallest new house cost £50,000 so people were prepared apparently to tow their old house across country. At Fox Bay West the company had set up a small school some time after we had left which was closed 40 years later so they are back where they started. The Government proposed to provide a travelling teacher, one week in five as it had in 1944. The only new thing is the back up of this kind of education by video and improved radio. Although Land Rovers and the like are now available and there is an air service it sounds as if the basic problems created by isolation remain the same. It is hard to believe that subdividing the land which can only raise sheep is likely to improve the standard of living for more than a very few and may perhaps cause unemployment.

The article states, "Almost none of the new owners are in a position to offer employment."

Port Howard too is facing radical changes; there is now a small hotel where the Pole-Evans used to live. I don't know which would have upset the old man the most, the farm being subdivided or his home offering bed-and-breakfast to all and sundry. These all seem to be enterprising attempts to inject new ideas and new life into the camp and one can only hope they will succeed. One lady a new owner occupier in Fox Bay West referring to the old system was quoted as saying.

"It was a sheltered life but the only way out, if you were ambitious, was out of the Islands."

This must still be true. Taking into account the miniscule population, the poverty of the land, one would expect that only the ambitions of a few can be satisfied.

The winter of 1944/45 was not severe, but, nevertheless, it did not encourage outdoor pursuits. I used to busy myself in the surgery warmed by an oil stove. I had various supplies of medicines to make up to fulfil standing orders for cough mixtures, antacids and optimistic remedies for rheumatism. I amused myself by varying the flavours and, in an unguarded moment, the colouring of medicines on order. Stupidly I failed to keep a record of the colour of individual prescriptions. Patients used to ring me up and complain that their latest pink medicine was nothing like as effective as the previous bottle I had sent. Then I had to try and discover what colour the previous lot had been without them realising that the active ingredients were precisely the same, no matter what colour red, green or purple.

Since we were a young, newly married couple with a small baby we did not suffer as much as might have been expected from social isolation. Apart from our new domestic responsibilities, Shirley's with Penny and planning meals and food supplies and the like. Mine in the meat house and coping with exasperating oil lamps' eccentricity. We took up photography, and I continued half-heartedly with my correspondence course pending our re-entry into a wider world.

In the summer that followed, we were suddenly stricken with a whooping cough epidemic which, not unnaturally, confined itself to those stations visited by the Fitzroy on a particular voyage. I introduced a voluntary quarantine system for the West Falklands which was strictly observed and no cases occurred outside the originally infected area. This was one occasion at least where difficult communication was really a benefit.

In the quarantine area, there were 111 people who were contacts. The previous epidemic of whooping cough had been 20 years before in 1924. Everyone over 20 years old claimed to have been infected in the previous epidemic. On this basis, I calculated that 52 cases might occur. In the event, there were 47 cases, an attack rate of 90%. Unfortunately for us, Penny was one of the victims of this really unpleasant childhood scourge and sometimes she was very ill indeed. This was well before the great days of the triple vaccine, but, as now, once the disease has been contracted there was nothing we could do but ride out the whoops as best we might. It was a very distressing an anxious time and Penny might well have succumbed to the disease, which is at its most dangerous at the age she was then. As it was, it was months before she stopped vomiting and losing weight. Feeding her became a major exercise which continued throughout her childhood. In fact, for about three years, she was left with an explosive cough, which distressed us all.

The quarantine lasted more than three months, the Fitzroy only called at ports on the west outside the quarantine area and mail was brought on horseback by an insusceptible courier. Several shepherds who had lived all their lives in the Falklands told me that whooping cough would be followed by mumps and then measles. When I enquired why they thought, so, I was told, in all seriousness, that whooping cough causes the other two maladies! Actually, this had, indeed, been the sequence of events 20 years before. The prophecy was eventually fulfilled since mumps occurred in considerable numbers in 1946 and was followed by measles in 1947. This long period between epidemics of childhood diseases are a common feature of small, isolated, closed communities and particularly of small Island groups. Whether this common experience includes the same sequence of events, I don't know, but it is not to be expected. I don't know what happened in the early 1960s or 80s perhaps there have been too many intrusive events, an invasion, occupation and then reoccupation to disturb the pattern of the epidemics. These events restricted our activities for some time. I made several short visits to shepherds families, though there were no cases of any great medical importance.

Meanwhile, in 1945, the war in Europe was fluctuating back and forth, but none of the sometimes worrying aspects, including the Battle of Arnhem, changed our absolute conviction of an Allied victory. So our first summer was taken up with consolidating our marriage, and looking after Penny and finding things to do in and around the settlement. The weather became marginally warmer and at the same time markedly windier, for the first time we began to realise what Malvinas really stood for. For instance walking to the Clement's house, 400 or 500 yards away, in the wind which blew at gale force or near it at least half of the time, you could literally lean on the wind, especially when suitably dressed in a sheepskin coat. We heard stories of cowsheds being blown out to sea, like Judy Garland's house in the Wizard of Oz. I actually saw a small shed being blown across the paddock leaving the ground for almost a minute. On one occasion, I watched a dinghy, which had not been properly secured on the jetty davits, swinging violently in the wind, being held up at right angles for seconds at a time and then crashing down time after time. It took three very strong men to fasten it down. There could be no doubting the quality of the wind.

The wind, together with the temperature of the water, icy cold all the year round, restricted swimming, sailing and fishing both commercially and recreationally. I occasionally fished for rock cod from our pram dinghy but only in very secluded parts of the creek. Our fishing was done with a line with a hook baited with meat and was really quite successful. I preferred to fish from one or of the other small cliffs overlooking one of the minor creeks where in the evening when the light was right, you could easily see where the fish were. They were mostly red mullet, usually about a pound to a pound and a half and very good eating. Fox Bay faced almost exactly due south so when the wind was from Antarctica, not only was it very cold, but the tide did not go out, so the creeks were sometimes full for days. After a few days, the wind would abate the water go rushing out. To take advantage of this phenomenon, the local lads had fashioned a series of fish dams in the creek. When the tide went out, if it had stayed higher for a day or more then the dams were often full of fish. All you had to do was walk along the fish wall select the fish you fancied and then shoot it with a .22 rifle. Naturally this was easier said than done, an empirical calculation of the refractive index being necessary, it was an effective if unsporting method of fishing. Throwing in thunder flashes or any form of explosive was very much frowned upon not so much because it was cruel and unsporting but because it was wasteful.

Falkland Islanders were always concerned about their food supply. Many thought it ridiculous to attempt to shoot geese on the wing when it was so much easier to shoot them on the ground as they spent a lot of time grazing like hens. There were occasions when I shot geese from the sitting-room window using the windowsill as a gun rest. I regret to say that we found the young females far and away the best eating. The geese had come to be regarded almost as vermin and there was a bounty of a penny a beak paid by some farmers to anyone who killed them. There were unfortunate methods which thoroughly upset the

Wildlife groups then and would create no end of a furore today. Since the geese at certain times of the year, because they were moulting, could not or would not fly, they would be herded into corrals and then slaughtered by hitting them over the head with clubs or whatever was handy. Whether there was any justification for this view I don't know but many of the farmers believed that geese ate the most succulent and therefore the most nutritious grass and thus were a threat to the sheep. On Weddell Island some years before the owner, a rancher living in Argentina decided to fix the geese once and for all. He imported a pair of Patagonian foxes from the Mainland and let them run. It is not difficult to imagine what happened. The geese disappeared all right, they simply flew away. Weddell soon became plagued by marauding packs of foxes which started by killing the lambs, then attacking the sheep and eventually riders on horseback. When I visited the Island they were paying half a crown a head for dead foxes, 30 times as much as they had previously paid for the geese. A penny wise and half-a-crown foolish you might say. For years Weddell could only manage a 5% lamb marking which meant that by the time the lambs were due for castrating and their tails docking in December only 5% of the lambs had survived.

At Christmas time goslings were very much sought after and, together with baby lamb, were regarded as a much greater delicacy than turkey. The goslings would be no more than a few weeks old, to kill them with a shot gun or any firearm would do far too much damage. On the Falklands they had adapted a South American Indian weapon, the Bolas. This consisted of three heavy balls or rocks, often covered in hide, joined together by a rope or strips of hide and then thrown at animal's legs to entangle them. This method was often used against cattle and rhea, the South American ostrich, but it was too heavy and clumsy against other birds. The knuckles of cattle were used instead of the heavier balls or rocks and in skilled hands, were very effective against goslings. I once saw six goslings caught in this way with one throw. This was on a small pond. The Bolas was skimmed across the water, as close to the surface as possible, with a circular action so that, as it rotated each knuckle extended as far as its rope or strip of cowhide would allow. In this way a large area was covered and escape minimal.

In the summer time we had visitors. The most fascinating

were the penguins who established a rookery only about 20 minutes walk from our house. There must have been a hundred or so Gentoo penguins and they were with us rearing their young for about six weeks. They chose a reasonably flat piece of land within easy reach of the sea and each pair set up a small territorial area where the nest was built. The male and female birds took it in turn to incubate the eggs, usually not more than two pretty large affairs. The male would do most of the fishing. It's a marvellous sight seeing penguins in the water. On land they're so clumsy yet in the water they have such freedom and enjoyment of sheer movement.

We were told the penguins were the fastest things in the sea and I would be quite prepared to believe it. The penguins did not seem to mind our visits and Shirley who cannot resist birds or animals, was soon able to stroke them, using a degree of care to avoid beaks and flippers. It sounds unlikely, I know, but she managed it. The professional way to hold a penguin is by the back of the neck and the end of one flipper. I have seen it done but never tried it myself. The nests were never left unattended and one could easily see why. If the mother just roused herself to stretch her webbed feet around the nest some bird of prey would swoop menacingly out of the sky when a few seconds before there was nothing at all to be seen. The swoop was accompanied by a screech clearly designed to unnerve the victim. The penguins never hesitated they were always ready to protect their own. We never saw the rookery attacked by seals this may have been because of the sitting of the nesting area. The seals had the reputation of being the penguins' worst enemy. Once having caught one the seal would throw the penguin high in the air holding its skin with its teeth in the process with the result that the poor wretched creature was skinned alive.

There were all sorts of creatures around Fox Bay and in the summer, we were privileged to watch the mating behaviour of a sea-lion and his clapmatch. One day we were walking along the coast which was indented with many small bays and creeks when in one sandy bay, we came across a pair of large seals romping around the beach together. We watched them for some time but it was several days before we realised what was going on. The sea lion a large eared seal with massive shoulders and a mane very like a lion's, was simply preventing his female companion, they were not yet married, from getting into the water. The clapmatch was about to produce a pup conceived by a previous husband met the year before as is the way with these animals. The lady was desperate to get back into the water and the sea-lion was equally determined that she should not. He won. He was much bigger and fiercer. The clapmatch was bloodied all over the back of her neck, evidence of his aggressive behaviour. We learned later that this performance was to avoid her giving birth in the water because if this were to happen the pup would drown. The pups have to be born and kept on land until their parents have taught them to swim and fed them with stones to provide ballast. Seals do seem to have difficulty knowing which way up they are. We went out most days to watch this family drama. One day there was the pup and we were able to see it daily thereafter until it was about 2 feet long. By this time we had been told what to expect. Apparently the two adults meet in the sea when the pregnant clapmatch is approaching the time of birth. The male brings the female ashore, provides food for her and stops her going back into the sea until the pup is born. When the pup has been trained to swim the two adults mate, all three of them then swim out to sea, say goodbye and never meet again. A rather lonely sort of tale which I hope, for their sakes is not quite true.

We had been told that the bigger seals could be dangerous and that when we were watching our seal family, we should not get too close. Apparently the sea lions will often chase people away and if you are on horseback, they might lurk in the grass suddenly rear up and grab the horse's tail thus tending to send the horse berserk with unpleasant consequences to the rider. Nothing like this happened to us. In any case, we were able to observe the family from a shallow cliff-like parapet which gave us a close view without intruding on the animals' privacy.

Watching the penguins and seals and their relatives gave us hours of entertainment and sometimes excitement. There was in Fox Bay at that time a villainous leopard seal which for a year or two had prevented the salvage of a scow load of wool that had capsized and sunk in the middle of waterway. A diver had been sent to Fox Bay to consider the prospects of recovering the load. Unfortunately someone told the driver about the leopard seal and that was that. He refused point blank to dive. As far as I know the wool and the scow remain at the bottom of the sea. The leopard seal was the fiercest of our local marine inhabitants.

Long before I was apprised of this potential danger, I was quietly rowing across the bay one day when there was a loud snort and an enormous creature appeared at the stern of the boat with the evidence intention of coming aboard. This was the leopard seal and I was quite simply terrified, although I didn't think he would make it into the boat I thought it not impossible that we might capsize. The thought of being in the cold water with this monster lent strength to my arms and I shot across the bay as if I was stroking the Cambridge eight. The leopard seal followed with immaculate ease gave me a few more snorts to encourage me to maintain my efforts. I don't suppose the animal was anything more than curious, but a curious half ton of blubber was something I did not want to share the boat with. All seals are curious and there were times when we enjoyed being escorted by the smaller variety with their graceful antics but not by the leopard seal. I met the latter once on land and could see how bulky he really was, with his grey-like appearance and spotted neck. Even on land he was an aggressive animal though his speed was curtailed, so he wasn't anything like as menacing as he was in the sea. Short regarded the animal as an unmitigated nuisance and I had to restrain him from shooting it on at least one occasion.

All seals were protected by law, but it was often rumoured seal poaching and smuggling still went on. There were recent tales about catches of sealskins left in out of the way places. One farmer who was asked to store barrels of salt pork thought that after six months he should check whether the meat was still sound. He discovered the pork was only a foot deep; the rest of the barrel was full of sealskins.

There was a sinister story about seal pirates some years before. A single-masted schooner used to sail from Stanley on a variety of missions some of which involved seal hunting which put the master and the crew in the pirate category. This activity was suspected, but to catch the pirates in the act or with the booty proved impossible. Eventually, the captain and crew fell out, allegedly over the division of the spoils, so they decided to make one final strike and sailed for the Jason Islands a remote group of rocks off the northwest extremity of the Western Falklands. Here there was no anchorage and the captain landed the crew to catch and skin the seals. While this was being done he sailed up and down the islands just offshore and when the work was completed he was later accused of taking up his gun and picking off his three-man crew one after the other. He was arraigned for murder, but subsequently acquitted by a jury too overawed to find him guilty.

Our final wildlife preoccupation concerned a blue whale washed up by the sea five or six hundred yards from our house. No one could say what had befallen the unfortunate creature but it fetched up right on high water mark so it was from our point of view very accessible. It continued to be a source of interest for at least three months and we would visit the site several times a week. This enormous carcase, it was 58 feet long, proved an even greater attraction to swarms of sea birds especially a species allied to the albatross. The latter would enter a hole often in the whales belly and totally disappear for quite a long time. Eventually they would emerge satiated and gorged with food and totter about in what appeared to be a drunken state. Many of them trying to take off would crash into one of the few fences which frustrated their attempts to fly. Locally this albatross like bird which had a very large wing span was known as a "stinker" because when landing o n the deck of a ship it would vomit in order to lighten its weight to enable its wings to take advantage of the wind since wing flapping for this purpose was not in its repertoire. These birds on land were lumbering idiots but once in the air they transformed into elegant gliders with intelligent use of the winds so that there was practically little need for wing movement. Fascinating. In about three months the whale or rather its corpse had gone. For the most part eaten by the birds but we always wondered about the bones high tides probably washed them out to sea. However two of the vertebrae provided stools for our sitting room and quite comfortable seats for Penny.

CHAPTER 10
TWO DEATHS

VE-day. A tragedy in Port Howard. Another on Weddell Island. Two very different sea journeys. My only visit to Saunders Island.

By the summer of 1945, the war in Europe was clearly approaching its end and there was increasing excitement after the Yalta conference, as events seemed to tumble over themselves. Then a series of deaths. Ironically the first was that of President Roosevelt, to whom we owed so much although, at Yalta, he may have left a fateful legacy. This was in mid-April followed at the end of the month by the shooting of Mussolini and his mistress and next incredibly to us then, the death of Hitler, apparently by his own hand. VE day finally happened one minute after midnight on the eighth of May.

The eighth of May must have been a Tuesday, the Sunday before, on their day off; the men in the cookhouse in Port Howard were beginning to celebrate the end of the war in Europe. It had been raining a lot, so no one was interested in visiting. Cookhouses were often larger than needed, so that visitors could be put up and extra men taken on during shearing or lamb marking time. The cookhouse in Port Howard was a large, double-storied building, consisting of a main room, used mostly for recreation and as a dining hall some rooms were off the main hall and others at a higher level on the next floor.

At about six o'clock that same evening came the familiar five rings on the telephone. I had been listening to the radio and rather expected it might be Wick Clement, the farm manager, wanting to discuss the news and perhaps split a beer. It was a farm manager Douglas Pole-Evans from Port Howard son of the doyen of the farming community, soon to be a member of Legislative Council. I knew very well that he wouldn't be ringing to discuss the war. Nor was he. There had been an accident in the cookhouse and a man had been badly burnt. When I heard the details I knew it was serious since the poor man lost, by the sound of it, more than half his skin surface. I told them what to do with their limited dressings, to avoid removing any clothing attached to the skin, wrap him carefully in a clean sheet and put him to bed but otherwise to disturb him as little as possible, fluids but no more alcohol, and then I remembered that they had some tincture of opium in their medicine chest .I told him to measure 20 drops of the tincture and give it to the old man. I said this would relieve the pain and with any luck allow him to sleep. If he was still in pain and restless after three hours or so the dose could be repeated. I could visualise him quite well and knew that although he was in local terms pretty old, he was also fairly robust, so he might just have a chance.

I think by this time my guide had changed to a very much younger man Alf Perry, a good guide and an excellent horseman. So the horses were rounded up in record time. We got to the rendezvous point on the mountain at Black Shanty way ahead of the man from Pot Howard, it was pitch dark and we dared not go ahead as we might miss him on the trail, since there were several which could be taken across the hills. When he did arrive, the delay was explained, a couple of hours earlier he had been met by a shepherd, who lived off the track, to be told that Jim Simpson had died.

I was not surprised and as it turned out the old man had lost an enormous amount of skin and many of his burns were deep and damaging. This was part of the recurring nightmarish dilemma any isolated medical practitioner has to live with. True, the isolation in this instance was extreme because the Fitzroy was in Montevideo, so hospitalisation would have been out of the question. I had to make it a rule not to plague myself with worrying about a patient till I had actually seen for myself. All I used to do on the telephone was to obtain enough information to decide whether a visit was necessary and then get going as quickly as possible.

We spent the rest of the night in the shack on the mountain, there were just two rooms, both fairly full of sheepskins, so it wasn't difficult to find somewhere to sleep. In the morning....and after a quick cup of coffee I rode on to Port Howard getting there fairly early on the morning before VE day. It was a very wet track. There had been a lot of rain, though I seem to recall that the morning was reasonably bright. I had forgotten that I was a Justice of the Peace until Pole-Evans Senior reminded me. So, after I attended to the dead man, I could not sign a burial certificate until an inquest had been held. This involved the elder Pole-Evans and me...and everyone else from the cookhouse was lined up for evidence.

We sat....as a Coroner's Inquest - in the main hall at a table - usually a dining table! Our backs merely a few feet from where the deceased had burned himself to death. Pole-Evans was irascible and bad-tempered.....reflecting his dismay and regret at the death of someone he had known and worked with for twenty years or more. The questions were routine and obvious but asked in an accusatory manner by Pole-Evans, which I tried to tone down in order to get answers from the overawed witnesses. Each witness had been in the cookhouse on the day of Jim Simpson's death. Every one of them felt guilty because he had been left alone. All felt nervous and alone.

As it so happened, the only radio in the cookhouse at that time was owned by one of the men who had his room upstairs. So it happened that all the men - bar Jim Simpson - were gathered around intently listening to the BBC News. At the time, Jim was shut off from the main room quietly drinking his rum and smoking his pipe beside the fire in the kitchen. Not a particularly lethal occupation - one might think. It seems that he had drunk more than he realised and also had spilled a good deal of the contents of the bottle down the front of his clothes. He then attempted to light his pipe and, in his befuddled state, dropped a match. This would not have been serious had he not been using "camp" matches! These matches were normally used for burning grass at winter's end .in order to make way for new grass. One could strike them riding along on horseback and throw them into dry grass. They burned far longer than ordinary matches by virtue of a combustible head a centimetre or so long. In this case such a match proved disastrous!

Embarrassing and difficult though the interrogation proved to be the facts were clear enough so we brought in a verdict of 'accidental death'. The funeral took place the same day, which caused greater embarrassment since, in the rocky soil, digging the grave was more a matter of bailing out flood water. In fact, the only way the burial could be completed was by weighing the coffin with sufficient boulders to sink it!

The population of The West Falklands at that time….was between 4 and 5 hundred people only. During our time on the West, we only had two deaths. We had a young community - both deaths occurred in people over 60 years of age and neither one could have been prevented. I remember…..years later……asking a postgraduate student whether the death rate in hospital would be higher or lower than the death rate of the area as a whole. The question was considered to be unfair, since the answer could not be found in a textbook. In many places…where patients habitually are hospitalised when their lives become endangered…naturally the rate is higher. On the other hand, in some poor countries where treatment in hospital is paid for, then when death is inevitable, the relatives take the sufferers home to die. This explains the reason why, for many years, many cases of rabies were recorded in Addis Ababa…with very few deaths (even now, there is no cure for rabies).

The second death occurred months later - it involved the most extraordinary journey I ever made. An older man - reported by wireless- to be seriously ill with violent abdominal pains on Weddell Island far off on the West Coat and only accessible by sea. The Fitzroy was unavailable, .probably in Montevideo or perhaps even on the rocks! The only possible means of reaching the Island was on a cutter which plied the coastal areas of the Falklands. It was arranged that I should board the cutter somewhere close to Spring Point, on the west coast which at that time was part of Packe Brothers station which meant that Wick Clements the manager would supply both horses and guide. It wasn't far about three or four hours ride from Fox Bay West I was by this time more or less acclimatised to the horse, so this presented no difficulty. The problem was a storm was blowing up as we rode across the island and by the time we reached the boarding jetty, there was a gale blowing. This did not deter the small boat owner, or his mate, who both said it would merely ensure a fast passage since the wind direction was ideal. We covered the distance in something like two and a half hours, which was acclaimed a record time. Record it may have been, but it was highly uncomfortable, like riding a backing horse all the way, the boat rising and falling in the most unlikely directions all at once. I sat in the cabin, more or less opposite a lighted Dover stove, an old fashioned cooking grate designed to burn almost anything. I thought we were more in danger of dying from fire than drowning, especially when live coals shot all over the cabin floor and had to be picked up and thrown overboard. The noise of the sea and the wind was deafening. How the skipper found his way I don't know. .There were no navigational aids of any kind. Fortunately, I do not get seasick, nor was I then at all afraid of the sea, but I was apprehensive from time to time when the bows rose high in the air and seconds later crashed into the trough of the waves. It was exciting but I and the other two men on board were far too concerned with keeping ourselves and each other from being thrown into the sea..

In a very short time, the excitement was over and everyone was waiting at the jetty to witness this well-nigh historic arrival. Then I received the melancholy news that my potential patient had died. This time I was able to assert that the patient had certainly died of natural causes and I could and did sign a death certificate. Death was due to a perforated gastric ulcer and the poor man had had a lot of pain before he died. He had been sick with stomach pain and discomfort for years and his premature death might have been avoided if he had not lived so remotely on Weddell Island. I remember contemplating briefly what I've would have done if he had still been alive on my arrival. Evacuation of the patient to Stanley would have been quite out of the question and whether I could have achieved anything worthwhile with scant equipment, no facilities and no assistance whatever is highly doubtful. Nowadays, the patient would have been in hospital within less than two hours by helicopter but this type of medical emergency aid would at that time have cost more than the total budget available to cover all the Government's health responsibilities. In any case there were no helicopters or anything else that flew.

Arriving too late was a common enough occurrence. One day I received a message to say that three fires had been sited from Saunders Island by a shepherd on the Hill Cove station. There was no telephone and no wireless communication and the farm manager of Hill Cove station told me that the three flares signified a request for the doctor. I asked, I remember, how many times the signal had been seen. Only once, I was told, since the wind had got up and no fires could be seen or contact with the island made until the wind moderated. This island was also just about as far away from Fox Bay as it was possible to get and entailed quite complicated changes of guide and horses and at least one night stop on the way. I arrived at the manager's house in Hill Cove where as always I was warmly welcomed and invited to stay the night. Apparently there was no possibility of establishing contact with the island because the wind was far too strong and so flare signals were not possible. I suggested that I should just go and not bother about any further communication.

The manager grinned. "How do you reckon you are going to get their, Doctor?"

"Well," I said, "By boat I suppose."

"The boat has to come from the island. We don't have a boat on the mainland, not there at any rate."

I raised an eyebrow.

"You see, Doctor, I know it doesn't look far from the mainland to the Island, but it takes two men a good 2 ½ hours to cover the distance in fine weather, there is a constant east-west current of about 10 knots which makes the passage impossible when the wind is blowing."

I began to feel frustrated not to say nonplussed.

"So what do I do?" I asked

"Well, our shepherd will send a smoke signal just as soon as he can to say you are waiting to visit. When he gets a reply he can phone us here and you can then ride over to the pickup point which you should reach about the same time as the boat arriving."

"How long will that take?" I asked.

"A day or two may be. You are very welcome to stay with us here in fact that's what you will have to do."

In the event, I waited three days. Eventually the boat was promised and I set out to ride over, met it exactly on schedule, and after a really difficult row arrived at the settlement. The manager was politeness itself.

"We are delighted to see you, Doctor, whatever are you doing here, and why have you come?"

I told him.

"We don't have any need for a doctor. No one is ill." Then he paused.

"Wait a minute. Jimmy Smith did send smoke signal 3 or 4 weeks ago but nothing happened, so we assumed no one had seen the signal."

"So, what happened to Smith?" I asked

"Well, he had a bit of a fall and said he thought he might have broken his leg. He limped about a bit but he was all right in a couple of days."

"Do you realise I have come all this way and been away now for four days for something that never really happened?"

"Well, of course, Doctor, I am very sorry about that; but it is so nice to see you. We haven't had a visit from the Doctor here before, not as long as I've been here, anyway."

This disarming remark couldn't be resisted, so I suggested that I should meet as many people as I could.

"You can certainly see everyone on the settlement, but there are only four families and not many in the cookhouse. As to the other shepherds, they are too far away altogether. You see here we have to think of the weather all the time. You'll all be all right until tomorrow afternoon but any later than that we might not be able to get you to the mainland. I have had visitors stranded here for a week or more and though we should love to have you, I know you might be needed in other places. In short, doctor, I would feel much happier if we get you going by midmorning tomorrow."

I agreed to this and spent a very interesting time visiting everybody on the station. As usual, there were very few problems or even potential ones. My main interest was really focused on the pregnant mums or potentially pregnant ones. In these remote places, especially with first babies it was always as well to ensure that adequate arrangements could be made and transfer to Stanley organised well before delivery was due. No antenatal care could be provided, so it was sometimes necessary for the women to move three months ahead of time.

About this time we were invited to a wedding on the other side of the island where a young shepherd was marrying a very young girl. This was quite unusual since men would normally wait until they had saved up enough money to provide for a wife. They will also aim to marry someone who could cope with a shepherd's lifestyle though I would guess they would goggle at the thought that "lifestyle" applied to them. On this occasion, we all rode over to Chartres and stayed with the Luxtons for the wedding Shirley didn't ride very often, but she had had riding lessons at school and everyone was fascinated not only by her smart riding gear but also seeing somebody posting on horseback in the approved English fashion.

"She can't keep that up very long, Doctor," said one of the guides.

Of course he was right. After about twenty minutes the posting was abandoned. Shirley rode Bachelor. He was the most comfortable and quietest horse we had. Unfortunately, he constantly broke wind as he trotted along, so in this respect he was far from quiet and Shirley rode alone behind everybody else.

About a week after the wedding, we had five rings on the telephone and here was the bridegroom in urgent tones asking me to come at once, his wife was in terrible pain and he was afraid she might die. Naively, I questioned him about the pain its origins, whereabouts and so forth. A voice broke in on the conversation:-

"She's pregnant, Doctor. Having the baby right now I shouldn't wonder"

This indeed was the case and then, and only then, the penny dropped. So this was why they were marrying so young and this was why she had spent the whole of the reception sitting down clasping a whacking great bouquet in her lap. When I arrived some three or four hours later, it turned out that the telephone eavesdropper was dead right. The baby a full-term bouncing boy had arrived ahead of me. When I saw the relieved and somewhat tremulous patient, I discovered that the afterbirth had not yet separated, although the child was some three hours old. I tried all sorts of things, but the blessed thing would not shift. I remembered my old teacher, Greene-Armytage at Hammersmith telling us to avoid manual removal at all costs. This was in the days before antibiotics and puerperal sepsis was still a postnatal hazard. I also remember him imply that, skilfully applied force was sometimes necessary. The upshot was that I climbed onto the bed and forced the placenta out with the sole of my stockinged foot. Unorthodox, may be, but I was mightily relieved at its arrival. Mother and baby did well.

By 1946, a new Senior Medical Officer had arrived and he visited us in Fox Bay. His Canadian predecessor of the blankets and the post-mortem had left unheralded on promotion to the South Seas. The new man was much more affable and socially inclined and certainly seemed an improvement. By this time, we had more or less completed our tour in the West and the last few months were spent in euphoric contemplation of a return to the real world of Port Stanley with its population of perhaps 1500 people. Gosh!

I had not previously visited Port Stephens, the furthest most southerly point in the Islands until the Robertsons were transferred there from Pebble Island. Since I had spent a week with them at the very beginning of our time in Fox Bay, I regarded them as old friends. This time it was the manager's wife Nan Robertson who had a problem. She was an Australian, though I can't remember whether her husband was or not. He certainly had the figure for it and wore large hats. Nan was a character all right but formal occasions, which were virtually non-existent, tended to unnerve her a little. She had been known, for instance, to turn up with only one rouged and powdered cheek.

Rather late one night, an apologetic but worried Charlie Robertson rang to say his wife had a high-temperature with what sounded like a nasty infection of her left thigh. I knew she was the last one to make a fuss, so I made preparations to ride the following morning. The ride would take five or six hours as long as the weather held. Early the next morning, just as I was about to start on the ride to Port Stephens, Douglas Pole-Evans called to say that his father had had a very nasty fall late the night before and had come down heavily on the iron fender in the office. Now Port Howard was five or six hours ride to the north and Port Stephens five or six hours ride in the diametrically opposite direction. This dilemma I had often thought about but had not before actually been faced with it. I queried Douglas very carefully about his father's symptoms and judged that, at worst, he might have cracked a rib but had probably not actually broken it. I got him to write down carefully how to strap his father's chest to reduce movement to a minimum. Eventually I was satisfied that he knew how to do It. Then almost as an afterthought, I said,-

"Oh, Douglas, you still have about half a bottle of tincture of opium left, you know, the stuff you gave old Jim Simpson."

"Yes, I remember."

"Right, if you give him 15 drops of that it should ease the pain and he should sleep well."

Then I added,

"I am just about to ride to Port Stephens to see Nan Robertson and I may well be away for a week or so. I don't think the telephone from Port Howard will reach Port Stephens so, if you need anything, you must get the wireless operator to send a message. In any case I will get in touch with you as soon as I get back."

Not really a very satisfactory solution but I was pretty sure that the old man would be all right, especially after a few days rest. The ride to Port Stephens was pretty dreary, the land had been flat and uninteresting, though the weather was good and it was merely a matter of riding out the hours. The Robertsons were their usual hospitable selves and Nan progressed well. She was actually the first patient to be treated with sulphonamides on the West Falklands. I had been quite shocked when I first arrived to find that the stock of M&B tablets was so very limited. I had been accustomed to use them without much thought in Whipps Cross Hospital, especially for lobar pneumonia. Later, in Stanley, their use was jealously guarded. The odd sailor with Gonorrhoea was reluctantly treated, being regarded as unworthy, this complaint being more or less self-inflicted. Even then we had one or two cases from Buenos Aires who showed resistance to the drug.

My stay in Port Stephens was all the pleasanter because the Fitzroy was due and I could take passage as far as Chartres on the Luxton estate and ride home from there. When we left the creek protecting Port Stephens, we ran into the worst weather I had so far encountered on the Fitzroy and, even after a mammoth breakfast (I don't remember whether it included fried brains) I was only slightly queasy for half an hour or so. On the way to Chartres we called at New Island one of the smallest of the inhabited islands which was also one of the most attractive. The Fitzroy anchored in the small but beautifully symmetrical bay in the lee of a rounded hill. At night the ship went on loading under a searchlight and lit up the hill which suddenly turned into a Christmas tree with flickering lights. The hill was the home of hundreds of small birds living in holes in the ground. They had fluorescent wings and evidently the light caused them to flutter from one hole to the next. Whatever the reason, the result was magical and a sight to be seen. New Island was also the home of masses of penguins as constantly entertaining as the small birds. There was a colony of king penguins and I suppose now, with the Falkland Islands unbelievably on the tourist circuit, New Island must be a high spot, if not the high spot, for the adventurous tourist. If it is not it surely should be.

One family had lived on the Island in total isolation without visiting the mainland for 16 years. An idyllic existence as long as it lasted, but there were two daughters and so when eventually the inevitable happened and the family entered the hurly-burly life in Port Stanley, the result was a social workers nightmare. All this happened much later, after we had left to return to Europe, but at the time it was as near to paradise as one can imagine. Hell it seems is always just around the corner.

When I disembarked at Chartres I was able to speak to Port Howard on the phone. I had not had much doubt that old Pole-Evans would have recovered, but I was relieved to get confirmation from his son Douglas.

"He's very much better, Doctor. He says he can't manage without the strapping, which he won't let me take off. I think he can, he hardly ever remembers to say it's hurting."

"Well, that's fine Douglas, I should just leave it. It'll come off in the bath before too long."

"Oh! He hasn't had a bath since it happened."

"Right, so you'd better tell him I said he must have one now or he'll finish up with dermatitis."

Then I remembered he had used some of the Tincture of Opium and I kept a check on those sorts of drugs. So I said

"By the way, Douglas, how much Tincture of Opium do you have left in the cupboard?"

At this, he became a bit evasive. He wasn't sure, but probably about the same as when I last looked in the cupboard. Then a thought slipped into my mind.

"Douglas, how many drops did you give your father?" All Roundheads and Cavaliers!

"Well, er," he began to stutter "Not much, well actually, I didn't give him any at all."

"Why ever not?"

"I didn't like to!"

"What?"

"Well, Doc, I was afraid to. You remember what happened to poor old Jim Simpson."

Chapter 11
Port Stanley Again

Return to Port Stanley. Prophetic visit by HMS Uganda. I escort Governor to Montevideo. I win at roulette.

Quite suddenly, our time in Fox Bay came to an end. Somewhat strangely I was relieved by someone I knew, David Arthur. He was the cousin of a constant companion in my early days as a medical student at St Mary's, when we both lived in Ealing. Anywhere less like Ealing than Fox Bay it would be hard to imagine. We enjoyed a few days together handing over since the Fitzroy was going around the Island and would return to Fox Bay before going back to Stanley. David and his wife Robina had a very small baby and it was like looking back at ourselves and our own arrival in Fox Bay twenty months earlier. Such isolation for newly qualified doctors such as we both were, though David had more experience in medical practice than I, should not have happened even given that there had been a war on. I, professionally, lost almost 3 years working more or less alone through a period which should have been the most intensive learning period of my career. It was true that I was in a sense self-selected but I would lay odds that no record on my file drew attention to the fact that I did not really intend to choose the Falklands. Bureaucracy never achieves a sense of humour, and anything written down in a file is sacrosanct.

In spite of all that, neither Shirley nor I regretted our time in the Falklands or even Fox Bay. I learnt to be independent and was forced to be self-reliant but there's no doubt looking back that my early days turned me away from clinical medicine and made me a bit of a loner. My later experience in Uganda where I was also professionally isolated made matters worse or perhaps it was better.

We left Fox Bay in April 1946 almost 2 years to the day since we had left Liverpool. I don't think either of us was ever homesick. We were both only children and had both left our parents homes years before we got married. So we were accustomed to rely on friendships we made as we went along, and very good friendships many turned out to be.

In Stanley we went back into the same house we lived in briefly before and tried to come to terms as quickly as we could with the social life we were obliged to enter. As newcomers to a limited social circle, we were in great demand. His Excellency the Governor Sir Alan Wolsey Cardinall was still in Government House. He rang up our house one morning and spoke to Shirley welcoming us back to Stanley.

"I am going to give a dinner party, I want you both to come I have a very special treat. I have managed to get some green peas to go with the eternal mutton."

"Oh!" Says Shirley. "How lovely I haven't had a pea since we came to the Falklands."

Then she stuttered a bit in confusion at the realisation of what she had said. She accepted the invitation hoping that he had missed the double entendre. But he had not. After the soup HE at the dinner party , for twelve people, serving from the end of the table solemnly placed one pea on an empty plate and instructed his butler to put this in front of Mrs Hopwood. This was duly done.

The Governor grinned all over his face,

"You can't say you haven't had a pea in the Falklands now can you?" Said he.

The work I had to do was quite different and naturally more interesting. Most of the time I looked after all the outpatients and my boss the new SMO looked after the patients in the hospital. Just before I arrived there had been an anaesthetic death so I was a little apprehensive to hear that two operations were awaiting my arrival. In the event these passed off safely certainly as far as the anaesthetic was concerned, thank goodness. Otherwise I was, in effect, the GP for Port Stanley and I enjoyed it especially the opportunity to meet all sorts of people, although the total numbers at that time were only about 1400. These did not include members of the British armed forces since the war was over the Army personnel were rapidly being repatriated. There were still naval personnel because Stanley was a semi-permanent station and they ran the metrological station amongst other things.

The Army had a dental surgeon, who was loaned part-time for civilian work at the hospital. This was Jimmy Tomlinson, who became Colonial Dental Surgeon after his discharge from the Army. He and his wife Winnie became our best friends and we spent most of our leisure hours together either in our house or theirs. The level of friendship we achieved with the Tomlinsons for our remaining time in Stanley was never quite repeated anywhere else. Sadly it did not survive for long. After we both left the Islands, we went abroad again and they stayed at home. Nevertheless we kept contact for several years but eventually distance and time took its toll and we never recaptured those carefree days in Stanley over the bridge table or Mah Jong.

At that time in Stanley, it was easy to make friends since we all depended on each other for relaxation and recreation. We had no TV and no cinema, although the Town Hall (rebuilt by now) showed films on the odd occasion. The radio reception was poor and we seldom were able to listen to anything other than the news programmes. Occasionally we had visits from warships. In particular, I remember one such visit from HMS Uganda which was about to be decommissioned and become HMCS Montreal. She was about to join the Canadian Navy and actually had a Canadian Admiral on board who played a banjo-ukelele and sang what I think we called hillbilly music. Whatever it was, it was a great treat and we all enjoyed those visits enormously. This may have been a somewhat prophetic visit for, in a short time, we were to find ourselves living in Uganda. I am not even sure whether I had ever heard of it before. I do remember looking it up in the Atlas to see exactly where it was.

One certain thing about His Majesty's Overseas Civil Service, which was created just after the war, was that constant change was the order of the day. Sir Alan's days as Governor came to an end quite soon after our return. He had pretty severe diabetes and was really very ill. I was deputed to accompany him on the first leg of his journey home. So it came about that I was back on the Fitzroy in charge of the Governor as far as Montevideo. Since he was so ill, he spent most of the time in bed, but continued to be a most entertaining companion. He was also kind enough to take an interest in my future.

"Now, young fellow, you have started pretty well. It is always important to keep your name in front of the authorities. If you do everything by the book, keep your head down and never get mentioned, that is the surest way to oblivion. In the Navy, the best way to promotion is to keep on sinking your ship".

I hadn't realised before, that he had a cynical turn of mind!

"That business of yours with the blankets - good idea - long drawnout correspondence with the Colonial Office - just the thing. You won't come back to the Falklands, of course, but you never know what they might offer you at the end of your tour. There are many wonderful places to go and work".

I remembered him telling me of his own days in the Gold Coast and the Cayman Islands and of his early adventures as a reporter in Vancouver. He had been knighted when he was Administrator in the Cayman Islands which didn't rate a Governor in those days. It was difficult to realise that the Falklands had been a promotion. For years, the Falklands was a consolation prize for the worthy but uninspired. Its main importance being as a supply and communications point for the British possessions in Antartica.

Then he said:

"One thing you must never do is work in South Africa. It is the most beautiful country but the Boers will take over the Government and there will be trouble. They will certainly leave the Commonwealth".

At that time I had given little thought to my future. I had no objectives, other than to learn and then earn sufficiently to keep the family afloat. Nevertheless, I have never forgotten those conversations on the way to the River Plate. South Africa left the Commonwealth in 1961 and, by then, its Government had committed the extreme folly of establishing Apartheid. So, Sir Alan's remark was pretty far-sighted, since this was in 1946 and apartheid did not come into being, at least officially, until 1948 or thereabouts.

The voyage to Montevideo was uneventful. When we got within the River Plate waterway, the sea was flat calm and grey, with a mist closing down. Against this background, there was the oddest storm I have ever experienced. It was hardly a thunderstorm - no wind, no turbulent clouds to be seen anywhere - the noise of thunder was muted somehow. But all around the ship, for an hour or so, were forks of lightning diving directly into the sea. It was the most eerie ocasikon and gave one the feeling that the lightning might strike the ship at any moment. I never actually heard the hissing of lightning meeting the sea. Perhaps it doesn't hiss!

When we reached Montivideo, we were greeted as celebrities and whisked off to the Hotel Del Parque in Poscitos - the posh end of Montevideo and part of the South American Riviera. Today, the hotel would have had a 5 Star rating on any classification. My bathroom was larger than our bedroom in Stanley. Sir Alan, of course, had a suite. Seldom had I seen such magnificence and was duly impressed, to say the very least. It was early evening by the time we arrived and the Governor elected to go to bed.

"When you've settled me in, you go off and enjoy yourself with your friends. There is no need to cosset me. I shall be perfectly all right".

I took him at his word and went downstairs. The stairs eventually swept into a marbled foyer and walking down the final steps was like being in one of the Hollywood-style movies which tried to make you believe that everyone in the USA lived in a palace. Across the foyer, my friends were waiting. Ted Allison from the Royal Mail office was there with a couple of his colleagues, and Don Clarke, the General Manager elect of the Falkland Islands Company who was on his way to Stanley for the first time.

I was greeted with cries of:

"Good, here's the Doctor now. How's the old man? Will he let you off the leash?"

"I think so - but I'll go up soon to see how he is - I think he will be glad to be on his own for once".

"Great - we plan to go bowling later at the Tupinamba. What'll you have to drink?" The waiter was hovering and took the order.

I remembered the Tupinamba quite well it was I think on. the 25th May Avenue - which only sounded right in Spanish - Avenida Veinte Cinco de Mayo. Shirley and I had been there one night on our way through two years earlier. It remained empty until about 10 o'clock at night and then, during the week at least, it filled up with men only, as a café where people were just as likely to have coffee and cakes as aperitifs. They had very odd working hours in Montevideo - starting quite early in the morning and then closing completely in the afternoon from about two to seven in the evening - then going back to work until 10 or 11 p.m. when all the bars and cafes came to life and remained so until the early hours of the morning.

The waiter brought my drink and said something in Spanish to Ted Allison.

"The waiter has asked if you would please give him a prescription for his rheumatism"

"Oh dear!" I replied. "Tell him, I'm sorry I cannot give him a prescription in Uruguay because I'm not on their medical register"

That was a pretty naïve remark. I didn't realise at the time that you could buy any drugs you wanted over the counter at any Pharmacia in Montevideo, provided you were able to pay for it.

We happily chatted away - the locals trying to decide where would be the best place to eat and then we had another drink. Halfway through my second drink, I decided it was churlish to refuse the waiter's request.

I turned to Allison.

"Ted, would you tell the waiter, I will give him a prescription for the Rheumatism, on condition that he gives me three numbers for roulette at the Casino tonight".

I had already taken a brief look in the casino at the hotel and, although I knew nothing about gambling or any of the games played there, I had thought roulette might be fun.

The idea intrigued the waiter who busied himself finding paper for me to write his prescription. He was a youngish man and showed no signs of rheumatism, so I supposed the medicine he wanted was probably for his mother. Anyhow, I wrote him a simple prescription for a Salicylic acid mixture which was standard at the time.

The waiter produced a little English.

"Esta noche, tonight Senor, the casino she close at one, uno in the morning. You go at half-past twelve, not before. At half-past twelve only, comprende?"

"Yes," I said.

"You play only on table numero ocho, not before half-past twelve".

"Very well" I replied.

"Then, Senor, los numeros, you play only six, eleven and fourteen".

I must say he put on a good show, all flashing eyes and gesticulating hands. It was all quite dramatic. He finished by wishing me luck and thanked me profusely for the prescription. He shook me vigorously by the hand and would certainly have kissed me had I not remained firmly seated!

After this incident, we went off somewhere to eat and arrived at the Tupinamba for the bowling. This was not an American bowling alley but much more like the English type of skittles. There were only nine skittles and they were smaller than the modern ones. There was no automatic system to pick up the pins, but a young boy appeared from behind the scenes and reset the skittles whenever necessary. It was good fun and, before I knew it, it was after midnight and I was in danger, like Cinderella, of beikng late home. I insisted on going back to the hotel and, when the others were less enthusiastic, I called for a taxi, but in the end, we all went back together.

By a minute or two before 12.30 a.m. I was in place at table number eight. I had decided I could afford to lose £5. Not much, you might think, but it was getting on for £500 at today's rates. The rate of exchnge was 7 pesos to the pound sterling and each chip was worth one peso, so I was standing there with 35 chips in front of me. 12.30 came and went and so too did the chips, three at a time, on 6, 11 and 14. At about quarter to one, I had five chips left and was resigned to losing the lot. Only briefly did I think of cashing in the last five, so on I went. In the next fifteen minutes or so, till the end of the session, the numbers came up eight times. Everything happened so quickly I had a job finding pockets for all the chips. I was wearing a waistcoat at the time and, for a day or two afterwards, I recovered odd chips from previously unused pockets. I don't remember the exact sequence of events but, fairly early on, number 14 came up twice running and an enormous pile of chips appeared in front of me. I almost protested that I had been paid too much, when one of my friends pointed out that, when I had won the previous time, I had left the original stake on the table so, for that turn of the wheel, I had been betting two chips, not one! This happened twice, so I ended up more than £50 in pocket. Although I tried to find him, I did not see the waiter again. I could only hope the prescription cured his or his mother's Rheumatism.

I spent a good deal of the next day shopping in style at the big departmental store, London and Paris. I was escorted round the store by an English-speaking assistant, who, in fact, had an MSc in Engineering, but the best job he could get was that of a floorwalker in the store and he got this because he spoke English, not because he was an engineer. I spent all the winnings on presents and clothes for Penny and Shirley - It was amazing what you could buy in those days for what now seems a very small amount of money. The gifts included a wooden indoor swing for Penny and also a small slide similar to the ones you see in a children's playground.

All this time, I was checking on Sir Alan's condition at the hotel and arranging for someone to keep an eye on him after I had left, since we were sailing before his ship was due to take him back to the UK. I had developed qujite an affection for him by this time and could see perfectly well that his days were numbered. He was returning to live by himself in a flat in somewhere like Leamington. How he would manage on his own, after being waited on hand-and-foot in Government House, was hard to imagine. The answer was, of course, that he didn't - for he lived only a short time after I left him in Montevideo.

CHAPTER 12
THE STRAITS OF MAGELLAN

Rough seas. Punta Arenas a visit to a brothel. A new Governor arrives. Last days in Stanley.

I left the Governor in his sumptuous bed at the Hotel Del Parque knowing full well that I should not see him again, so the promises we made of meeting back in the UK must have sounded unreal to both of us.

We had had a good trip up from Stanley and indeed I had always been reasonably lucky with the weather whenever I was on the Fitzroy. The coming trip was to alter all that with a vengeance. The wind blew almost from the minute we entered the River Plate and the seas seemed to rise higher and get bigger by the hour. After a noisy and tempestuous night, there was nobody for breakfast in the dining saloon but me! In fact, my memory of that trip was almost as though I was the only one on board. I can only remember speaking to the Captain, who kept to his bed most of the trip - incapacitated by seasickness like most of the passengers. This was Johnny Johnstone, a tall, stiff-backed man who always seemed to be leanikng slightly backwards. He had recently been taken on from the Endurance, one of the Antarctic-going ships and I don't think he liked it much. No one liked the Fitzroy. I sat on his bed after a day or so at sea and said:

"I suppose she's safe enough, Johnny, isn't she? I mean, we're not going to lose a mast or anything?" He grinned sardonically and cocked a yellowish eye in my direction.

"Well, Doc, all I can tell you is that if she takes three seas running on her foredeck, she won't come up again".

Back I went to the wing of the Bridge and stood watching the waves towering above the little ship. I now knew what was meant when mountainous seas were talked about. Here they were. In the first onslaught, some of the glass windows on the Bridge had been cracked and the first wave that came smacking against the glass was usually the worst. I looked out on nothing but white cascading water. There was no part of the foredeck to be seen. Then you could sense the ship struggling to get up against the mass of seawater and, before she could manage it, down could come another wave and in no time there was another mass of white water threatening the deck. Just before it could land, the bows would shudder up and out of the water, just enough to catch a glimpse of the deck. Time and again this happened. I kept constant watch, almost mesmerised by the sight, so that on that voyage I only left the Bridge in the dark and for meals - solitary ones.

The Fitzroy used to chug along at a steady ten knots, but on this trip we only achieved 150 miles one day and 90 the next. She should have been covering just over 240 miles. Johnny, when he was making ujp the log, remarked that he was pretty sure most of this was backwards. The voyage took 2 ½ days longer than it should. On this trip, we were not going directly to Stanley, but calling at Punta Arenas first. Eventually, we entered the Straits of Magellan and I remember thinking that, when this happened, the weather would moderate and everything would be more comfortable.

I had been given the Director's cabin on board. This was on the top deck and looked rather like a summer house, with windows all the way round, shrouded by thick curtains. It really was very nice, or would have been had the weather been anyways decent. This edifice was bolted to the upper deck just in front of the funnel. The first time a wave hit it, I practically fell out of bed. I inspected the bolts carefully each morning checking for any sign of play or weakness. I did not fancy finding myself bobbing about the waves of the South Atlantic in mid-winter.

Our passage through the Straits was very impressive. I lay in bed in my gazebo with the curtains drawn right back and what a sight it was! By this time, not only was a full gale blowing, but there was a snowstorm as well. In spite of this, the water itself was relatively calm. We made little progress and it became so difficult to maintain course that Johnny the Skipper said he wished we could anchor until the storm had blown itself out. The sheer sides of the Straits towered above us on both sides and apparently the depth of water was such that there was not enough anchor chain to reach the bottom. Lying in my bunk, the snow was blowing exactly parallel to the water and a great snowdrift piled up on the windward side of my little cabin. It became very hazardous indeed going to the dining saloon or crossing the deck at all.

Punta Arenas, when we reached it, was frozen solid. The roads were glacial but there were very few cars and one had to walk everywhere. The English Club was a refuge of leather armchair comfort. We stayed ashore at the local hotel while the ship went across the Straits to collect Patagonian wool and presumably deliver stores from Montevideo.

I remember practically nothing about the hotel except that it was undistinguished in every respect, including the food. One evening, Don Clarke and I found the meal so unappetising that we asked for Tomato Ketchup. This caused some supply problems, but eventually, the sauce bottle was plonked on the table. When we came to pay the bill, the cost of the ketchup - the entire bottle - had been added onto the bill. Complaining didn't seem profitable, so we simply took the sauce bottle away with us.

When the Fitzroy returned, Johnny, the Captain, said the hotel and club were too boring and he would take us to a place where the drinks were good and it would be quite lively - so off we went - Johnny, Don and me. We slithered down several streets, the houses shrouded in darkness. We stopped at what looked like an ordinary bungalow and Johnny knocked confidently on the door. The door opened cautiously.

"Ah, Captain Johnny, come in, come in". Then behind she called "Este el Capitano".

At this, the whole place suddenly lit up revealing a largish room with a bar set out with a few tables and chairs. Apart from the bar, the room must have been like an ordinary Chileno sitting-room., which I suspect it was most of the time. Three or four largish women appeared from nowhere, dressed mostly in black with thick, thick legs and carrying all before them. They were very polite, serving drinks and the inevitable *fiambres*. One of these formidable women put on the gramaphone, the old HMV type with the handle and the dog watching the turntable go round. One of the women volunteered to dance, but neither Don nor I took up the invitation. Johnny to our surprise, danced around and seemed to enjoy it. We had another drink and both agreed we had had enough of this dreary place, but it was only then we realised that Johnny was no longer with us. When we asked one of the women (they were certainly not girls) where the Captain was, she gestured with her hands and said. "El Capitano, gone push-push - he will return pronto".

We were so taken aback that we couldn't get out of the place fast enough to avoid upsetting anyhone by bursting out laughing. We staggered outside and started sliding all over the ice, more-or-less on our hands and knees. Since we were laughing so much, standing was a problem. We were laughing at ourselves as much as anything. We simply had no idea at all that Johnny's "lively place" was in fact a brothel. Nothing was ever said about this night's advanture.

CHAPTER 13
RETURN

Last days in Stanley. Bridge at Government House. Aboard the SS Lafonia. Visit to Buenos Aires, Another Colonial Office interview. New appointment

On our return to Stanley, it was to find a new Governor in Government House and a 2,000 ton ship, SS Lafonia, in the harbour. This was to be the flagship of the Falkland Islands Company and she really did put the poor old Fitzroy to shame. It was intended that the Lafonia should do the trips to and from Montevideo and the Fitzroy should go round the Islands collecting the wool and delivering stores. This sounded fine and so it was for a while but, some few years later, when the price of wool had been hit by the advent of man-made fibres, the Lafonia was sold and the clock put back. She was a great acquisition at the time, with good-sized cabins and a deck for promenading and, in good weather, sitting gossiping over a gin and tonic.

Sir Miles Clifford, the new Governor, unlike his predecessor, was married, but I think his wife had a hard time adjusting to the dreariness of Stanley and felt rather isolated by protocol, which severely restricted the people with whom she could be friendly. She was of an imperious turn of mind and did try knocking the local ladies into shape, but with little success. As for Sir Miles, he was probably similarly depressed by the lack of colleagues and the loneliness of his position. We were only in Stanley for a short time after his arrival and we did miss the friendliness of Sir Alan Wolsey Cardinall.

As the time to leave grew closer we prepared for the journey with some impatience. Although the war was over, it seemed that the recruiting machinery of the Colonial Office had not improved and still functioned with Victorian propriety, preserving its august and mysterious authority. Thus it was not until a week or two before, we were actually due to sail that we heard that my replacement was about to be appointed. The inevitable happened and I had to stay until my replacement arrived. Shirley decided that she would take the opportunity to visit one of her old friends in Buenos Aires, a girl who had married a Spaniard in Barcelona and whom she had not seen for years. We were all packed up, so this seemed a good idea.

One good consequence of the delay was that I was able to meet my successor, Jackie Stafford, an ex-Olympic boxer for Ireland and pugilist for Trinity, Dublin. Jackie had been in the RAF in Iceland so he was really turning things upside down. In spite of his Irishness, which was emphatic, almost his greatest love was Scotch Whiskey, which was not even then in abundant supply, most Falkland Islanders relying on Brazilian gin and rum, both grossly over-proof, I might add. We spent about one month together because the Lafonia was otherwise engaged and, during this time, we cornered the whiskey market, not for profit but to ensure that Jackie would not be deprived. We also spent several evenings at Government House, playing bridge with the Governor. By this time, Lady Clifford had given up and returned to the UK. Jackie was not one whit disturbed by HE's eminence and regaled us, with his inherited charm and technique with many a raucous story. One remark I do remember was:

"She's what I wud call an old Bag, Your Excellency, if you'd pardon de expression, sor".

Even in such a small place, the Governors were treated with the greatest respect, so I did wonder how Jackie's genius for informality would make out. Since he relieved me years later in Africa, he must have managed all right.

About a month after Shirley and Penny had left, I found myself at the end of our Falkland Islands experience. When eventually, I embarked on the SS Lafonia, I had the first official day off since arriving. The trip to Montevideo with Sir Alan had been on duty - so I was resolved to make a holiday of the trip home. When I reached Montevideo, it was to discover that although, as a Government Servant, I had some priority, the Government Coast Agent was encouraging us to put off our departure and make the most of the opportunity to enjoy Uruguay for as long as we liked. My first task was to go in search of Shirley and Penny in Buenos Aires, so off I went on the River boat up the River Plate. We had a pleasant time in BA, but it was more-or-less midwinter, and the Argentinians had their recurring and persistent political problems. Evita and the Peronistas were then somewhere near the zenith of their popularity. Nevertheless, they had backed the wrong side in the war so recently over. We were warned that, whenever we were in a taxi or anywhere wherever conversation could be overheard, never to mention Evita or Peron since it would automatically be assumed that the remark would be disparaging and trouble would ensure. We never did, and it didn't.

We had taken only a limited amount of money with us to BA and, when it ran out, we determined to leave for Montevideo. The River Ferry travelled overnight going eastward, so it was quite late by the time the taxi left us on the dock to struggle with our suitcases and Penny's paraphernalia onto the ship. We had arrived about one hour ahead of embarkation time and queued up to present our papers. When we got to the head of the queue, our troubles started. The immigration officers/police were dressed in Gilbert and Sullivan uniforms, all bright blue and gold brade but, in spite of the comic operetta appearance, they treated us with unconcealed dislike. None spoke English, but eventually it was borne in upon us that we had no visas to visit Montevideo and so we would have to go ashore. This was a terrifying prospect, since it was pitch-dark, the dock was more-or-less empty and we had absolutely no local money at all. I protested as vigorously as I dared and was simply waved away. We sat on a couch watching the other passengers having their papers stamped, wondering what on earth to do. As we sat there, one of the white coated stewards passing casually by whispered:

"Go to the cabin, stay there until the ship sails. Lock the door, don't come out for anyone and don't speak".

So, off we went to the cabin, which was quite large. We locked the door firmly and waited in total silence with bated breath. We listened apprehensively to all the comings and goings, but no one banged on the door. The ship sailed and we knelt on the bunk so we could look out to make sure that we were well out in the river before we could relax a little. We still believed we might be refused entry to Uruguay when we reached Montevideo. Then a knock on the door……

"You can come out now" the friendly voice of the English speaking steward,

He took us back to the office where we had suffered our sinister interrogation. The same genlemen were now wreathed in smiles and full of welcome.

"So sorry, Doctor…..welcome…welcome", they even managed a little English. It appeared that the Argentinian police had been on board until the ship had sailed. They had spotted the Falkland Islands entry in our passports and this was the cause of the problem. The Uruguayan officials explained that they had to put up a show in front of their Argentine counterparts to prevent us from being carted off to the local lock-up in BA. The relief was considerable.

I had known that Falkland Islanders with passports from Stanley could never visit the Argentine. If you were male, between the ages of 18 and 45 and held such a passport, you would be conscripted for military service in the Argentinian army. We always regarded Argentinian claims on the Falklands as a ploy by Peron to take the heat out of local disaffection, particularly in the sphere of labour relations. The most uncomfortable time in Buenos Aires was in mid-summer, where the appalling humidity made working conditions almost intolerable and this was the time there tended to be strikes and demonstrations. To cool the political atmosphere, Peron would rail against Britain for what he claimed was the wicked and illegal occupation of the Islands. The Falkland Islanders never took this seriously, finding it hard to believe that anyone would really want to take over the Islands. Although so many were ambitious to leave, nevertheless, they were often fiercely defensive of any criticism of the Islands or the Islanders. Nobody I ever met really thought that the Argentinos had a valid claim and it amused the philatelists to collect the stamps from BA, which coloured the Falklands the same hue as the Argentinian mainland. To send a letter from Buenos Aires to Stanley (though during the war this could seldom have happened); cost the same as a letter to any rural area of Argentina. I never met anyone who had received such a letter, nevertheless, this belief was widely held. Certainly, no one living in the Falklands during the war would have believed it remotely possible that 40 years later there would be an Argentinian invasion. It looks as though exactly the same opinion was held in 1982.

So, perhaps we were lucky to avoid worse treatment, but we were very glad finally to get safely ashore in Montevideo and to feel among friends again. We stayed in Montevideo for a week or two until we finally got passage on a Royal Mail liner bound for Liverpool. This ship was crammed with steerage passengers returning to Europe. All these passengers were subjected to a medical examination, particularly for Trachoma, a disease of the eyes with which, at that time, I was unfamiliar. The voyage was in great contrast to our outward journey three years earlier. It took about two weeks only and we called at the Cape Verde and Canary Islands. There was no blackout on the ship and everyone was in festive mood. I cannot now remember, for the life of me, why we bought a carpet in Montevideo, but I do remember that everyone told us it would cost a fortune in custom's duty, because it was brand new. So, a week or so before the end of the voyage, we managed to get the carpet out of the hold and put it down onto the floor in one of the saloons. By the time we parcelled it up again, the carpet could truthfully be termed 'used'.

In the event, this was quite unnecessary. We were met, by prior arrangement, by a forwarding agent. He was a dapper little man dressed in a brown dust-coat and very matter of fact in manner.

"How long have you been away, Doctor, if I might ask?"

"Three years or thereabouts" I answered.

"Have you anything to declare?"

"Well, I don't really know. What has to be declared?"

"How many pieces of luggage do you have?"

"About 25 or 30, I think, and we did buy a few things in Montevideo".

"Right, you'll have to declare something with all that lot" says he.

He went through the list and marked off a few items and then suggested I should give him ten pounds. Then, as an afterthought, he asked if I had any butter. As it so happened, we had been warned by the agents in Montevideo that there was a shortage of butter at home and we had stocked up. We offered him a couple of tins of butter. That was the last we saw of him or our luggage, but the latter turned up faithfully a few days later at home in Yorkshire and we never did find out what happened to the butter or the money.

After the excitement of reunion with family and friends, although I had a long period of leave due, I had to think of the future. This process had barely begun when I received a summons to the Colonial Office for what would now be called debriefing, I suppose.

I had visions of a re-run of my first interview, but, as it turned out, this one was totally different. No large semi-circular table, no intimidating atmosphere and no unidentifiable mass of faces. This time I met the Medical Advisers to the Colonial Office informally, separately and together. There were three in those days. They were all very friendly and quite shocked to hear that I did not want to continue in the Colonial Service. They suggested that before I finally made up my mind, I should go on a course, any course. They even offered to extend my leave and pay allowances. They succeeded in making me feel wanted, but I was still doubtful so I responded by saying I had always wanted to teach Physiology and could I do a BSc in this subject and then teach in Mona at the University of the West Indies. I think they might even have tried if this were possible, but a week or so later, I was told that there were no funds left for such training. I had a final visit to Great Smith Street and was offered a place on the DPH course, starting in September, for nine months on full pay and allowances. I agreed to take the course without any obligation to continue in the Colonial Service and, to my surprise, they accepted this proviso. I joined the course at the London School of Hygiene and Tropical Medicine in September 1947. I thought that at least I would gain a qualification which would ensure employment in the Public Health services, mostly in those days run by Local Health Authorities, and at a time when the National Health Service was still only a Bill and not an Act. In the following January, I received a formal letter signed once again by the Secretary of State, offering me a post in Uganda as a medical officer. There were four medical colleagues from Uganda on the same course. I had become very friendly with one of them - Ian MacKichan, so over coffee, I asked:

"Ian, tell me, what is Uganda really like?"

"Well, all I can tell you is that it's the only place I know of where you can lead the life of a gentleman on a moderate income".

We lived in Uganda for fifteen years.

www.ingramcontent.com/pod-product-compliance
Ingram Content Group UK Ltd.
Pitfield, Milton Keynes, MK11 3LW, UK
UKHW041937190726
13854UKWH00004B/1644